INSIDE ARCHITECTURE

INSIDE ARCHITECTURE

INTERIORS BY ARCHITECTS

Susan Zevon

Photography by Judith Watts

THAMES AND HUDSON

First published in the United States of America by:
Rockport Publishers, Inc.
146 Granite Street
Rockport, Massachusetts 01966-1299
Telephone: (508) 546-9590
Fax: (508) 546-7141

ISBN 1-56496-278-4

10 9 8 7 6 5 4 3 2 1

Design: Sawyer Design Associates, Inc.
Designers: Diane Sawyer, Rebecca Sagen
Front Cover Photograph: see page 43
Back Cover Photographs: *(top to bottom)* see page 178,
see page 33, see page 105

House designed by Debora Reiser: Photographs on pages 148-157
reprinted by permission of House Beautiful, copyright © April
1996. The Hearst Corporation. All rights reserved. Judith Watts,
photographer

Loft designed by Michael Rubin: Photographs on pages 120-129
reprinted by permission of House Beautiful, copyright ©
September 1992. The Hearst Corporation. All rights reserved.
Judith Watts, photographer

Printed in Hong Kong by Regent Publishing Services Limited

ACKNOWLEDGMENTS

· · · · · · ·

THIS BOOK HAS, FOR MANY YEARS, been an idea in my head, a pursuit and a goal that withstood many reversals. Without the help of many talented and patient people it would never have become a reality. First of all, Judith Watts, whose photographs enhance this book's pages, and I thank all the architects whose work was an inspiration and who generously contributed to the project. We are indebted to their clients, who welcomed us into their homes and gave us insight into how the projects reached fruition. Our thanks to Jennie McGregor Bernard, who enthusiastically guided it through initial phases, and to our agent, Barbara Hogenson, who continued to believe in this book through many setbacks. We are very appreciative of the support of Rockport Publishers, Inc., who gave this book life, especially to the acquistions editor, Rosalie Grattaroti, who remained unceasingly enthusiastic about the project right from our initial conversation, to our editor, Shawna Mullen, and art director, Lynne Havighurst.

During the years of work I was blessed with many loyal and talented friends who were always there with advice and encouragement. They are too numerous to mention all by name, but in particular I thank Kaaren Parker Gray, the best stylist I know, who generously gave many innovative suggestions and much encouragement; Robert Lautman, a photographer and veteran of similar projects who lent his guidance; Ann Morris, who patiently listened to many late night conversations and always offered good counsel; Carol Moskowitz, a true, long-term friend; and Elizabeth Winchester, an accomplished interior designer and the best neighbor anyone could ask for. My thanks to the dedicated and supportive staff at House Beautiful, who took a great interest in this project and from whom I have learned so much during my years on staff; and to my first mentor in architectural journalism, Elizabeth Sverbeyeff Byron.

Most of all I thank my loving family: my sister, Barbara Zevon Berlin, and my brother-in-law, Donald Berlin, who generously gave their support and professional skills to this book; to my kind and wise nephews, Geoffrey Berlin and Eric Berlin, who have been a great source of advice and laughter; and above all my dear parents, Rhea and Louis Zevon, to whom this book is dedicated with very great love.

CONTENTS

· · · · · ·

FOREWORD

· · · · · · ·

HAVING BEEN THE EDITOR of several magazines that report on architecture, design, and decoration, I am particularly interested in the way architecture works, inside as well as out. I like not only to be able to "read" the interior from the exterior forms of a house, but I love to study the floor plans and see how the network of rooms and passages come alive as beautiful, personal, individual environments.

No wonder I was delighted to discover that a colleague of mine was working on *Inside Architecture,* a book on interior design by architects. Here would be a book that would look at houses as I do, not only as a form in a landscape, important as that may be, but also as a complex composition of spaces, objects, and artifacts, as well as personal taste and style. And the author is an architectural editor I know very well.

I first met Susan Zevon in the 1970s at *House & Garden* where she was assistant editor for architecture. Later I became editor-in-chief of *House & Garden,* and Susan joined the staff of *House Beautiful* as architecture editor. Ultimately I became the editor-in-chief of *House Beautiful,* where my work with Susan continues to this day.

She shares my passion for houses and, as this book will reveal, her years in the field have taught her that no one vision dominates it. There are many design points of view to *Inside Architecture.*

The rooms architects create for themselves, as well as those they design for other people, include an amazing variety of visual and aesthetic experiences. For designers like Buzz Yudell and Tina Beebe, a house is clearly a place for comfortable living in close proximity to nature; for their mentor Charles Moore, houses and their interior spaces were exuberant exercises in *joie de vivre*; for Charles Gwathmey, architecture is an opportunity to work with the beauty of classic modernism;

while Robert Venturi and Denise Scott Brown embrace broad choices in both design and decoration.

Some of the examples in this book push the stylistic envelope, many of them found in urban lofts and other new forms of residential architecture. Examples include the work of younger designers like James Hong, Frederic Schwartz, and the Hariri sisters, Gisue and Mojgan.

Still others are more traditional: the home Peter Pennoyer created for his parents, the house Lee Mindel designed for himself, Hugh Newell Jacobsen's work for clients and his own family.

But then, as Hugh Jacobsen's introduction to this book reminds us, the tradition of architects orchestrating all aspects of a house goes all the way back to Robert Adam, continues through the arts and crafts tradition of the Greene brothers, to the work of Frank Lloyd Wright, and his polar opposite, Ludwig Mies van der Rohe.

Whatever the design point of view, we can all learn from the way architects handle the interiors of the houses and apartments they design. And I, for one, never tire of the variety, creativity, and originality Susan Zevon finds in her coverage of architecture, and that she and her photographer and collaborator Judith Watts have documented for *Inside Architecture.*

Louis Oliver Gropp
Editor-in-Chief
House Beautiful

INTRODUCTION

· · · · · · ·

HOW DO YOU DESIGN AN EMPTY ROOM?
Everything an architect does, really, is concerned with
the making of spaces. The size and relationship of these
spaces is the result of predetermined programmatic
themes suggested (or dictated) by the client and the site.
The placement of furniture and the selection of colors
and fabrics are part of the design process, and, as everyone knows, it is a worthless effort that produces a space
without purpose.

The work illustrated in this book addresses interior
spaces designed as architecture by architects. These
spaces are appointed with furniture, rugs, objects, and
colors specified or designed by them as well. These
rooms are at peace with themselves because there is the
pervasive evidence of order. Without order there can be
no architecture.

The work herein is varied and personal. Some
interiors are sparse and some filled, but all are strong,
livable and innately beautiful. The architects of the
work shown are active practitioners, and the projects
included have been completed, for the most part, in the
past decade. Some of this work continues to evolve, as
architects are always moving and restudying the problem at hand.

It was not until the early Renaissance that architects were seen to turn over the interior shell of their
building to decorative artists. Still, the majority of the
great interiors in architecture's past were designed and
accomplished by the same architect that designed the
building. The work that was accomplished by these
architects influenced the times and often buildings
designed by others that followed them.

In order to create a sense of place, it is imperative
for the architect to be responsible for as much of the
visual environment related to the building as is possible.
Therefore, it is of little surprise that—historically—
most serious architects have designed their own interiors. A brief overview of those architects, whose special

contributions and influence have carried over the past
two hundred and fifty years and continue to the present
day, is, I believe, worth noting in this introduction.

The work of Robert Adam in late eighteenth-
century England was so thorough and so complete that
the results were judged "flawless" by contemporaries.
Through his efforts the rigors of Palladian neo-
classicism were made more linear and taut. Within the
spaces he encouraged and experimented with the play
of natural light. He boldly brought a new meaning to
interior spaces and their innate progressive relation-
ships to one another. From beaded and polychromed plaster walls and ceilings through the white and crisp sim-
plifications of Greek and Roman prototypical moldings,
fireplaces and surprisingly large windows, to chairs,
sideboards, beds, rugs and even chandeliers, Robert
Adam created a total and strong environment that
never contradicted itself.

For the first time, the architecture both within and
without became one. A comparison of this interior
exterior relationship and the unity created by Adam is
at the same time possible with the architecture of
France under Louis XVI. It was in seventeenth-century
France that "Interior Architects" first appeared. They,
of course, were trained architects who were specialists
in what the Renaissance had brought into existence: the
Decorative Arts.

The architect, who traditionally is responsible not
only for the exterior form and its proportion and scale
and the arrangement of the hierarchy of spaces within,
but also for the complete science of building, which earlier concerned itself with structure and being comfortably warm and water-tight, later took on the regimens
of the industrial revolution. It was not until the early
Renaissance that the concept of the placement of
objects and furniture began to be incorporated into the
architect's realm of responsibility. Prior to this time, the
design of the structure and its resultant spaces was the

chief responsibility of the architect. Overwhelmed, the architect encouraged and supported the arrival of a true colleague, educated and responsible for the interiors.

Thomas Jefferson, who was perhaps the last true Renaissance man, is a rich example of the architect's pursuit of total control. At Monticello, the ingenious doors, writing tables, beds, let alone the relationship of one to the other, are, of course, one with the architecture. The interior spaces and quality of light within fulfill the promise made by the view of the building when first seen from the approaching road. Monticello is one within and without—the brilliant effort of a brilliant architectural scholar turned amateur architect.

It is in the spirit of this book to recognize and refer to the influential work of the nineteenth-century American architects whose legacy is apparent herein. The contemporary efforts of Benjamin Henry Latrobe and the disciplines of the Greek Revival in the early decades of the nineteenth century express his concern for the continuity of purpose, from interior column capitals of corn and tobacco leaves through the scale and echo of this new order and into the furnishings themselves. The clarity and purpose of interior spaces, with light and scale of furnishings clearly reinforcing the order of solid and void inherent in Andalusia, the great house near Philadelphia, must be recalled at this time.

The endeavors of the highly creative and prolific architect Stanford White are perhaps the clearest example of the efforts architects have extended in their pursuit of their art. One can sense in nearly every Stanford White building the presence of his eye. The rich legacy of his work has been cherished beyond its brilliant execution of Beaux Arts disciplines to include spaces that are at once grand and simple, whose interiors are filled with objects that play off one another like a fugue. From picture frames, fabrics, furniture and juxtaposition of disparate forms, Stanford White's genius remains dominant and, a fact that is hardly surprising, still continues to carry the day.

The Arts and Crafts Movement, and it truly was that in both Europe and America in the late nineteenth-century, had an influence, though he denied it, upon the genius of Frank Lloyd Wright. It evolved in Britain in the 1880s and was a reaction against a century of mass production and the havoc it had wrought. It encouraged a revival of the concept of medieval guilds and hand-crafted objects of lasting beauty and utility. In England the leadership of Ruskin moved naturally through William Morris and almost immediately included the creative efforts of Charles Rennie Mackintosh, C. R. Ashbee and the classicist, Sir Edwin Landseer Lutyens.

Not surprisingly, the great American genius, Frank Lloyd Wright, breathed deeply of this creative air. From this, Wright created a design philosophy that he called "Organic Architecture." This was based on an underlying and essential unity of program, site, plan, elevation, structure, ornament, furniture and materials. This, not unlike Adam and the others above, led Wright to conceive buildings in their totality and, accordingly, he designed interiors, furniture, metal work, ceramics, stained glass, textiles, lighting, and murals wherever possible. The English Arts and Crafts Movement inspired the anti-urban, utopian guild spirit of the American Gustav Stickley in Syracuse, New York, whose work Wright privately espoused but publicly denied, as he did all possible influence from Japan, through Mayan, up to and including the Arts and Crafts.

The Viennese architect Joseph Hoffman, whose furniture is more well known than his few works of architecture, exercised control over his projects with the same purpose and intent that strong architects have been stressing in order to establish a complete visual order and, therefore, a sense of place and innate beauty. His furniture and interior spaces continue their influence nearly a century later and clearly echo the popular movements in design on both sides of the Atlantic before the Great War.

Between the World Wars, architects Ludwig Mies van der Rohe, Marcel Breuer, Peter Berens, Walter Gropius, Le Corbusier, and Alvar Aalto contributed architecture and interiors both recognizable and familiar to the theme of this book. Eero Saarinen, Charles Eames and George Nelson, to name only a few of the post–World War II architects, have not only contributed to our society and culture through their buildings, but through their design of furniture and interiors as well. The impact of mass production for a mass market drove these architects to wed the new technology with their architecture. Widely acclaimed and received by a broad populace eager for change, the efforts of these architects are now referred to as "classic" in the face of fashion. The fact that these same efforts were immediately accepted by the general populace and professional colleagues as "good" seems of less importance.

Today, the furniture and objects designed by Robert Venturi and Denise Scott Brown, Gisue Hariri and Mojgan Hariri, Charles Gwathmey and Robert Siegel, are broadly marketed to reach out beyond a single building and to bring that order and its beauty to thousands of other interiors. There is no question that the contributions made by these architects will continue to maintain the ever important contribution to our culture and society.

While most, if not all, the other architects whose interiors are specifically addressed herein design furniture, the chairs, sofas, tables, interiors, and furniture designed by Stanley Tigerman and Margaret McCurry, Michael Graves, Charles Moore and Arthur Andersson have made a strong contribution that continues and renews again the complete role of the architect. The study of the design of interiors and furniture by architects is the close-up study of the works of these architects. The fine detailing of this work is getting close to the core of their thoughts.

Architecture and design is a vast subject involving all of man's endeavors. It is important to understand that architects have always been designing not only the forms and resulting interior spaces but the color, furnishings and other objects vital to the concept and purpose of each building.

That the human figure is the most important object in a work of architecture is self-evident and is mentioned here only as a point of beginning in forming a philosophy, if you will, in the approach to the design of interiors. It therefore follows that the architecture and the inherent spaces within should be designed as backgrounds to man—backgrounds that make man look not only good, but better.

—Hugh Newell Jacobsen

ROBERT VENTURI & DENISE SCOTT BROWN

· · · · · · ·

Liberating Architecture

THROUGH THEIR WRITING, teaching, and design work, Robert Venturi and Denise Scott Brown have forged upon the landscape their vision of what Venturi proclaims to be the truth of an architecture of complexity and contradiction: a "unity of inclusion rather than the easy unity of exclusion." Nowhere is this vision more apparent than in their own home in suburban Philadelphia, where they have lived since 1971.

In the early years of their marriage, the couple frequently passed by an "almost art nouveau" mansion on their way to visit Venturi's mother, who lived in the house he had designed for her—now considered an icon of twentieth-century architecture. Completed in 1964, the small house signaled the revival of historical references, ornament, and color at a time when pure modernism was almost universally accepted as the only "correct" architectural style. With its tall chimney and large picture window, the design looks hauntingly familiar. The little house posed big questions: Why shouldn't a house look like a house? Could the popular also be art?

Two years after his mother's house was completed, Venturi's book *Complexity and Contradiction in Architecture* was published. It became a doctrine of liberation from the corporate glass box that had prevailed in American architecture since World War II. In the first chapter, "Nonstraightforward Architecture: A Gentle Manifesto," Venturi wrote, "I am for messy vitality over obvious unity. I include the non sequitur and proclaim the duality." Like the pop artists, Venturi and Scott Brown put the familiar in a new context, enabling us to view it with fresh eyes. Unlike many of their contemporaries who disdained decoration, they revived the interest in interior design that had characterized earlier architects. Today not only city plans and eminent projects such as the Seattle Museum and an addition to the National Gallery of Art in London bear the signature of Venturi and Scott Brown, but also furniture, rugs, and tableware.

Venturi describes their own house as a combination of Jugendstil, English arts and crafts, and the Continental art nouveau, a suitable choice for architects who "like elements that are hybrid rather than pure." Scott Brown and Venturi had been living in a one-bedroom apartment in I. M. Pei's concrete-and-glass Society Hill Towers, but in 1971, the arrival of their son, Jimmie, and the acquisition of four truckloads of furniture from Atlantic City's old Traymore Hotel (which was about to be demolished) made larger quarters a necessity. They heard that the "almost art nouveau" house was for sale, and it held a strong attraction for them both. Scott Brown liked being able to see right through the house to the vista of a 300-foot rolling lawn in the back. It reminded her of the broad vistas she had grown up with in her parents' international-style house in South Africa.

Puzzled by the mansion's ambiguous style, they discovered that the house had been built in 1910 to the designs of Milton B. Medary for a German family, who probably had requested something reminiscent of the houses they had known in Germany. Venturi and Scott Brown were at first intimidated by its size but reasoned that it could serve as both townhouse and country home. It would provide abundant room for the extended family they wanted to establish: a changing guard of architecture students to serve as "handy people," other helpers, friends, family, and an Airedale. "The house allows us to lead the life we do," Scott Brown says.

It took them ten years to bring the house back from its dreary condition wrought by someone the previous owner had described as a "famous decorator." They removed the "violent" wallpapers and sold all the "vulgar" chandeliers. The handsome architectural bones once again were revealed, providing a sympathetic setting for the sizable collection of hotel furniture, which

Venturi describes as "beyond art nouveau and pre-deco." Like the furniture he inherited from his mother, the hotel furniture also bore a childhood connection. As a teenager, Venturi had been friendly with the hotel owner's children and had learned about the furniture.

Once the offensive wallpapers had been removed, Venturi and Scott Brown found the painted walls a bit bland. Over the years, they and a retinue of young assistants stenciled the walls, adding layer upon layer of decoration. With time they acquired some art nouveau furniture, which they juxtaposed with contemporary furniture and objects. Many pieces were designed by themselves and by friends. They have continued to add paintings, sculpture, and layer upon layer of books, magazines, and catalogs so that the house visually resounds with Venturi's reply to Ludwig Mies van der Rohe's famous statement, "Less is more." "Less is a bore," Venturi wrote, and so he and Scott Brown have lived.

Venturi and Scott Brown have restored the original mission-style woodwork in the large entry hall. Wood-framed glass doors that face the front door open to the living room. Geometric stencils on the walls pick up the mix of colors from the Mercer tile floor, original to the house.

In a corner of the living room, a chair designed by Frederic Schwartz for Venturi and Scott Brown's son stands between a red chair designed by Venturi and an orange plastic stacking chair designed by Joe Colombo. A floor lamp by Louis C. Tiffany stands next to the art nouveau cabinet.

*The rich mix of furnishings in
their living room exalts Venturi
and Scott Brown's preference for
"messy vitality over obvious*
*unity" and exemplifies their talent
for "the difficult unity of
inclusion rather than the easy
unity of exclusion."*

ROBERT VENTURI AND DENISE SCOTT BROWN / 17

Dining-room walls not occupied

by the house's arts-and-crafts–

style cabinets are stenciled.

Country dishes are displayed on

wooden shelves.

In the dining room, chairs from the Traymore Hotel surround the oak table. The names of the couple's idols—architects and a few musicians—form a frieze on the dining-room walls above alphabet prints by William Nicholson.

A detail of the library shows exuberant stenciling—exotic flowering trees set against an intricately patterned background, topped by stars. The framed photograph is from Learning from Las Vegas.

Comfortable upholstered seating from Venturi's mother's house surrounds the centerpiece of the library: an art nouveau repoussé copper chimneypiece. A French art nouveau clock stands to the right of the fireplace.

JAMES HONG

· · · · · ·

Stepping up to the Future

ON A NARROW, DENSELY populated street on New York City's Lower East Side, a small, three-story building bears a sign that reads HOUSE OF CANDLES. The sign is a remnant of the building's former purpose: the manufacture of ritual candles for the Orthodox Jewish population that decades ago inhabited this now predominantly Hispanic neighborhood. Behind a grimy door, a steep flight of stairs leads up to a light-flooded loft. Colorful furnishings and finishes are of such originality that you might wonder if the stairway has taken you up to the future.

This cheerful space is home/office/laboratory and gallery for James Hong, a gentle, energetic architect who has purposefully pursued his singular vision of design since completing his architecture studies at the University of California at Berkeley in 1972. When he graduated, he found it a boring period for architecture in the United States; the corporate glass boxes being produced at the time did not appeal to him. He was more interested in the furniture and product design being done by Italian architects, so he left for Europe, where his experience working in Gae Aulenti's office clarified what he wanted to do. "I realized I could never be the sort of architect who would spend his career as a draftsman on large commercial projects. I need to design things on a scale that gives me total control, to create things that have personality."

When he returned to the United States, the New York gallery Art + Industrie was shifting its concept away from showing Italian design exclusively and toward developing the work of American artists. Hong started designing furniture for the gallery, and after a year and a half he decided to leave his job to devote himself totally to designing and producing his own work.

At the time Hong was sharing a studio with several of the gallery's artists, but he needed more space in which to design, produce, and display his work. When

he found the House of Candles building, it had been abandoned for years and was in dire need of repair. "When I moved in, there was neither heat nor hot water. The front windows were boarded over, and it was a very cold winter," he recalls. For the first month it was too cold to sleep on the upper floor that was to become his loft, so he slept in the storefront area, which he now leases to a theater company. He uses the basement as a workshop.

Slowly, doing most of the work himself, Hong set about putting in a heating system, fixing the window frames, installing new windows, and restoring the tin ceiling. He organized the space so that the kitchen and bath are toward the back, where there was already a rudimentary bathroom. He built a platform to enclose the gas and plumbing lines, and he placed the kitchen and bedroom next to each other so that one window would provide light for both. Because the window in the bedroom faces an exhaust vent from a meat market and would therefore have to remain shut, he put a sliding window in the ceiling to provide ventilation. Hong also installed a stairway that leads up from the kitchen to the platform above the bedroom. From there he can get up to the roof. On the side of the new bedroom wall, facing the living room, he built cabinets that provide ample storage without being obtrusive.

He left the front of the loft, with its wall of windows facing the street, open to accommodate his ever-increasing collection of furniture. The question of how to create a covering for windows that pivot open from the center and face the street was, at first, puzzling. His solution: screens that stand about 1½ feet away from the windows, suspended from curved steel tubes. They are created from parachute nylon tinted in pastel hues. The screens filter the bright north light that bounces off the white walls and the colorful floor. Hong filled and sanded the floors, painted them white, and then applied a rainbow of paint tints with rags, starting at one end

and working toward the other. A coat of polyurethane protects the painted finish. The last part of the loft to be completed was the kitchen. "Because the rest of the space was kept fairly neutral as a background for the furniture, I wanted the kitchen to be a brightly colored thing in itself," he says.

His furniture designs—dining table, entertainment unit, sofa, bar, and workstation—look unusual but function in an extraordinarily straightforward manner. The loft may appear complete, but visitors constantly encounter changes—new pieces, new arrangements. "If this place is ever finished, I'm going to learn to speak French and play the piano," Hong muses. Yet it is clear that, like a mini-universe, his home will always be a work in progress.

From a perch atop the platform over the bedroom, you can see across the length of the loft to the wall of windows facing the street. On the left, two chairs designed by Hong—one of bright purple anodized aluminum, the other of gray galvanized metal, painted wood, and cushions upholstered in a synthetic fabric—are arranged near the TV cabinet, one of his first designs. Hong painted the piano bright purple. He designed the sofa in front of the windows for an exhibit at Art + Industrie. On the right is a playhouse created by Hong for his three cats. The English racing bike, one of several that he uses for zipping across town, is a street find that he fixed up and painted turquoise.

In a corner of the living room is one of a pair of swing-open bars designed by Hong. The steel frame for a Barcelona chair, another street find, stands in front of a cabinet whose drawers open to reveal collections of articles and catalogs. The stealth airplane that has landed in front of the sofa was designed by Hong for a sculpture show entitled "A Propensity Toward War."

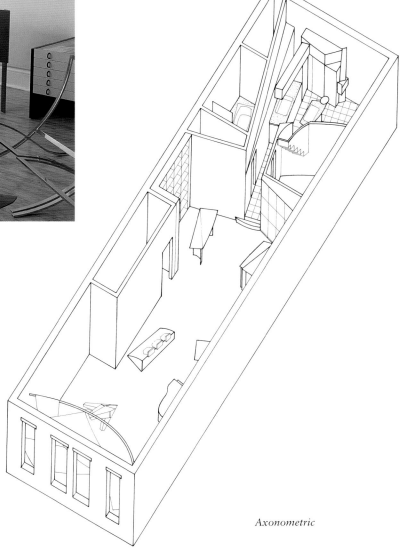

Axonometric

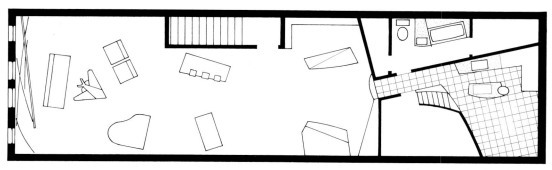

Floor Plan

Hong's workstation integrates all his office equipment: computers, fax machines, copiers, and even a built-in light box. The workstation is made of lacquered wood, vinyl upholstery, stainless steel, mixed-media cement, and tinted plaster. Hong found the Charles Eames–designed swivel chair and upholstered it in a faux leopardskin fabric. The tribal sculpture is African.

The dining table, designed by Hong for a contemporary furniture fair, is made of aluminum, granite, and steel, with a hand-painted surface. A corner was accidentally broken off, but everyone agreed that the missing corner seemed to be part of the design. Hong also designed the two screens, one of lacquered wood, the other of steel, that stand behind the dining table and chairs. On the left, the painting on glass is by Carmen Spera.

The back of the staircase that
leads from the kitchen to the
roof-access platform forms a
sculpture on the bedroom wall.
The painting above the bed is by
Chuck Glickman.

A refrigerator and microwave
oven are built into one corner of
the kitchen, alongside a little
countertop. The Piet Mondrian
print above the counter is a gift
from a grateful client.

Hong applied coats of dark and
light cement, finished with a
waterproof sealer, to the wall
surrounding the tub in his
bathroom. He placed a tempered-
glass partition with a hammered
texture between the tub and sink.
The stainless steel and copper
sink, also his own creation, is set
into a marble top.

A work island in the center of
Hong's Technicolor kitchen
contains a stove, a swing-out
wok, and a metal shelf that holds
hot plates and a kettle. The floor
is ceramic tile, the countertops are
black slate, and the wall above
the sink is steel that has been
burnished and sprayed with a
gold lacquer. The outside of the
cabinets is made from medium-
density fiberboard lacquered in
bright turquoise.

MICHAEL GRAVES

. . . .

Pioneering Postmodernism

OF ALL THE AMERICAN ARCHITECTS of his generation, it is perhaps Michael Graves who epitomizes the revival of American architects' attention to interior design. No other contemporary architect has produced such an extensive collection of home furnishings and objects. His own house in Princeton, New Jersey, has evolved into a reflection of his domestic vision and a show house for his designs. "A room is set up around furniture the way buildings are set up around landscape," he says.

His interest in interior design dates back to his school days in the Midwest, where he saw decorating being taught "next door" in the home economics classes for women. Later, after receiving his master's degree in architecture from Harvard, he worked in George Nelson's office, which, at the time, was producing furniture for Herman Miller. "I always saw furniture design as an extension of architecture," Graves says.

Graves entered the architectural limelight in the late 1960s as one of the "New York Five." His work,

along with that of Peter Eisenman, John Hedjuk, Richard Meier, and Charles Gwathmey, was known for its adherence to the influence of the international style and, in particular, the architecture of Le Corbusier. However, Graves's Portland Public Office building, completed in 1982, is often cited as the harbinger of postmodernism in architecture. Since then his name has become almost synonymous with the postmodern style. "Although Le Corbusier's buildings look great in the south of France, I began to have second thoughts about that architecture in this setting," he explains. "I wanted variety. I did not want all my buildings to look like refrigerators. My clients did not find the free modernist plan suitable to the domestic setting. They missed the ability to close a door."

The time he spent in Rome (1960 to 1962) as a fellow of the American Academy was seminal. There he studied the history and theory of architecture, disciplines that were not being taught at most American architecture schools at the time. The fact that Graves has never thought of buildings as distinct from their interiors he attributes to this influence.

In 1962, Graves started teaching at Princeton University, and two years later he opened his own architectural studio in Princeton. He was still a struggling young professor when, in 1970, he discovered an abandoned warehouse. Italian stonemasons who had come to Princeton to build the university's gothic-style buildings had constructed the storage facility in 1926, in a classically Tuscan vernacular using hollow clay tile, brick, and stucco. Attracted by its low price and romantic potential, Graves bought the warehouse and has lived in it ever since. Over the years he has worked on its evolution from a derelict rabbit warren of 44 interior cells into an elegant villa that increasingly reflects his passion for classicism.

He renovated the L-shaped building in stages, and first completed the north wing, where an entrance

courtyard that was originally a loading dock leads to a first floor comprising a living room, library, and garden terrace. A master bedroom and study are on the second floor. More recently, Graves has renovated the west wing of the building, expanding the kitchen and creating a breakfast room with doors that open to a garden, an exercise room, and laundry and storage space. A new staircase leads to a suite of guest rooms on the second floor. The rooms in both wings have been articulated by changes in ceiling heights, barrel-vaulted alcoves, niches, moldings, and columns. "When I design a plan for a house, I see it in three dimensions," Graves says. "Just as I like to see how characters change and plot unfolds in literature, I am interested in how rooms develop in sequence."

After two decades of work, the house has evolved into a live-in showcase of Graves's own designs and an enormous range of domestic artifacts: chairs, tables, light fixtures, clocks, picture frames, vases, and bowls are all displayed along with the classically inspired furnishings and objects he has collected over the years. The small icon of the postmodern movement, the teapot he designed for Alessi, has its place in the newly renovated, expanded kitchen. Like so many architects, Graves continues to regard his home as a work in progress. Future plans include transforming the living room and bedroom into a more expansive library and creating a new living room. The house has already matured into a stunning example of his vision for architecture and interior design.

ABOVE RIGHT:

At one end of the dining room, a
Biedermeier table and chairs
stand below a nineteenth-century
copy of Guido Reni's Aurora.

BELOW RIGHT:

In the dining room, Biedermeier
chairs surround an ebonized
federal period American table.
Graves designed the carpet and
lighting as well as the glass fruit
bowl with bronze armature, one
of his designs for Steuben. The
nineteenth-century candelabra are
copies of first-century Roman
bronzes.

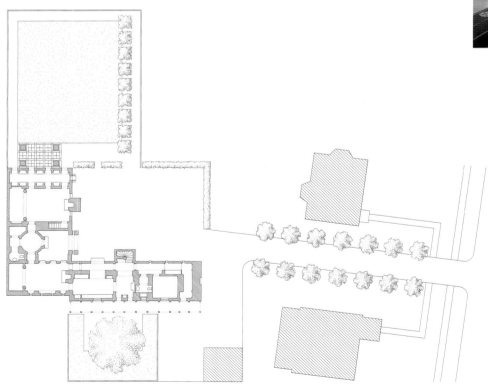

Site Plan

In the living room, some of the nineteenth-century Biedermeier furniture that Graves has collected is accompanied by his own designs. The lounge chairs near the fireplace were designed by Graves, and the glass flower vase with bronze armature is part of his collection for Steuben. The carpet is an antique chain-stitch Kashmir.

The view from a second-story light well is framed by an eighteenth-century architectural fragment purchased in Sorrento, Italy.

A nineteenth-century copy of a bust of a Roman warrior is seen from a second-floor staircase landing.

OPPOSITE:

The long, narrow library is flanked by elegantly proportioned shelves that, on the right, are separated by tall windows looking out on the garden. A nineteenth-century copy of a Pompeiian brasserie table stands below a circular etching in a gold-leaf frame designed by Graves. The carpets are antique Bokharas.

A transparent canopy fills the

two-story library with light.

North-South Section Through West and North Wing

East-West Section Through North Wing

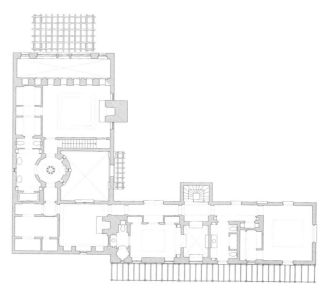

Ground Floor Plan

A rotunda with a glass dome graces the second floor.

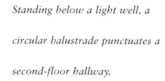

Standing below a light well, a circular balustrade punctuates a second-floor hallway.

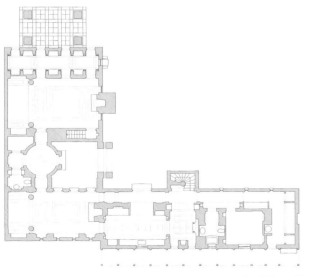

2nd Floor Plan

Doors open to the kitchen, where a nineteenth-century table, a local flea market find, stands in the center. Glass-fronted cabinets with old-fashioned drawer pulls flank a window that looks out on the garden.

In the newly renovated west wing, a breakfast room is situated adjacent to the kitchen. The French metal chairs, which have been faux-grained, stand beside a table designed by Graves. Shelves hold a portion of the Etruscan, Greek, and Roman pottery Graves has collected over the years.

In the second floor study stand a nineteenth-century Biedermeier piano stool and a desk draped with Fortuny silk velvet. A lounge chair designed by Le Corbusier occupies a corner. The carpet was designed by Graves.

In the newly renovated hallway of the west wing, a nineteenth-century, hand-painted Pompeiian wall fragment hangs above a nineteenth-century Biedermeier chest. The warehouse's original concrete floors were scored and painted to resemble stone. At the end of the hall, doors open to a guest bedroom.

In the master bedroom, a
fireplace is flanked by tall
windows that overlook the
gardens. To the right of the
fireplace, a bust (a copy of
Praxiteles' Aphrodite) purchased
from the British Museum
Collection stands on a nineteenth-century American
neoclassical pedestal. In the
corner is a Biedermeier chair.

LEFT:

One wall of the bedroom opens
to the library. Shelves display a
nineteenth-century bronze figure
and a twentienth-century French
painting of a view of the Seine. A

French empire table holds piles
of books. The bed is covered with
antique silks.

In the master bathroom, a nineteenth-century bench, holding a pile of towels, stands between a pair of late nineteenth-century porcelain basins. The floor is Rojo Alicante and Gris Di Quesa marble.

JOSEPH VALERIO

. . . .

Creating a Cultural Marker

WHAT DO YOU DESIGN for a client who, when asked to bring you images of his favorite places, presents you with photographs of Le Corbusier's Villa Savoye and La Tourette monastery and Frank Gehry's Schnabel house in Los Angeles? When Joseph Valerio was presented with these photos by Tracy Gardner, Valerio proceeded by doing an intensive, almost anthropological study of how Gardner lived, and he studied the site as well: 1,000 square feet on the 58th and 59th floors of a towering building in Chicago designed by Skidmore, Owings and Merrill. "You have to figure out how a person wants to live," Valerio says. "If the client is going to be happy, the space must fit like a glove."

A native of Chicago, Valerio did his graduate studies at U.C.L.A. and remained there after graduating to work with a group of older British students who were disciples of the British firm Archigram. Valerio was attracted to Archigram's work because "they were the first group to break with the modernist trend of the 1950s and 1960s to abstract materials. Archigram brought an awareness of materials and structure to modern architecture," he says. His work in Los Angeles consisted primarily of designs for movie sets, including some for Woody Allen's *Sleeper*. Valerio's experience in L.A. taught him "never to think that any idea was too outrageous." Another profound influence on his work is Robert Venturi's *Complexity and Contradiction in Architecture*. He still refers to the first edition copy he has owned since his school days.

When Valerio first returned to the Midwest from California, almost 50 percent of his work was residential. As principal in charge of design for the Chicago-based firm of Valerio Dewalt Train, he prefers doing only one residential project a year. "Houses are an architect's greatest challenge. They are a marker in terms of where we are as a culture," he says. The design for Gardner's apartment evolved over several months of

studying the client and the space. "The architects came in, opened closets, peered into drawers, and took pictures of how I lived," Gardner recalled. They showed him alternative schemes and listened to his reactions.

The apartment was a standard one-bedroom with a loft. All the walls were drywall, painted white; on the entry level, a staircase blocked sweeping views of Chicago and Lake Michigan; the bedroom and living room were side by side and of the same dimensions. Although there was only one bedroom, there was a bath and powder room on the main level and another bathroom upstairs. Nothing about the position of the functional services or window modules seemed to make sense to the architects. The apartment was dominated by the view directly to the north—an icon of Chicago architecture, the John Hancock Tower—also designed by Skidmore, Owings and Merrill. The dark monolith appeared to loom over the apartment, a stronger presence than the apartment's own walls.

The architect observed that Gardner, who often works at home, wanted to minimize the spaces devoted to what he calls the "messy" functions (sleeping, cooking, bathing, and storage) and maximize those devoted to "ceremonial" (conversation and contemplation). Valerio deduced from the examples of architecture Gardner admired that he was seeking a design that would be thin, light, and expressive of its materials.

Valerio decided to consider the apartment as a single space within its defining walls. Into this space, two boxes were inserted to contain the ceremonial spaces: an aluminum box on the lower level for entertaining and conversation, and a maple box on the upper level for the study. Because these were to be ceremonial spaces, the architects thought of them as "heaven," making their walls as thin as possible to express their ethereal nature. In homage to the strong presence of the John Hancock Tower, each of the boxes is "warped" by

the tower's imagined gravitational pull. The spaces between the boxes and the apartment's outer walls that were to contain the "messy" functions were named "purgatory," and the architect set about designing these spaces to conform to Gardner's needs. For his bedroom Gardner required only enough space for a sleeping alcove but wanted to be able to see the sun rise over the lake from his bed, so they pushed the bed as far to the west as possible and placed it right up against the window. The powder room and bathroom were combined to give him one large bath and dressing room. To give Gardner a large television that could be viewed from three areas—the bath, the bed, and the conversation area—within the limited space, the architects designed a media center and attached it to one of the pivoting metal panels that enclosed the aluminum box. Almost every surface of the two containers is hinged to provide access to the functional areas.

"The design allows me to live the way I want to," Gardner says. "Everyone who comes here is touched by it in some way. If they are moved by the view, they are moved by the design without realizing it." He admits that some guests are unsettled by the angles, and the way what they expect to be substantial is thin, but that does not bother him. "Art should affect your behavior and make you think. If it succeeds in doing that, it is good."

The leaning maple walls at
the entry frame the view of the
John Hancock Building, keeping
the rest of the apartment and
view a mystery until you step
further inside.

A wall of double-height windows opens the lofty apartment to an airplane-passenger's view of Chicago and Lake Michigan. The aluminum staircase leads up to the study on the loft level.

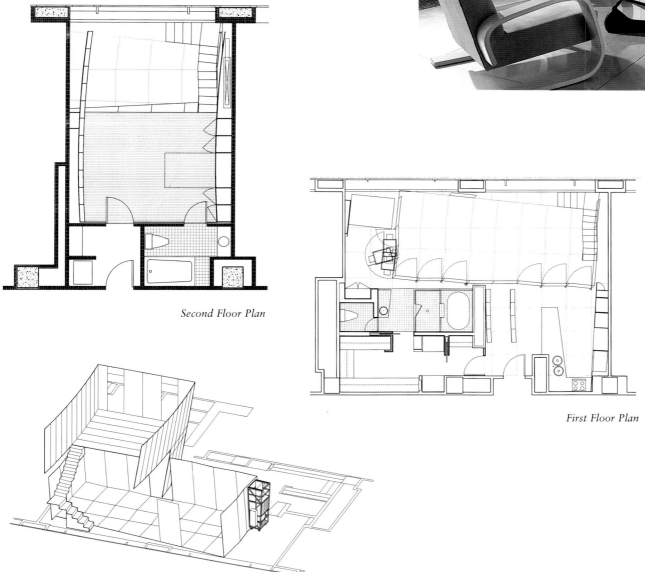

Second Floor Plan

First Floor Plan

Axonometric

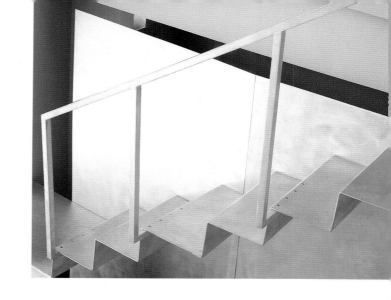

The aluminum staircase that leads up to the study is, according to Valerio, "so thin it defies description."

Aluminum panels contain the conversation area, which is furnished with classic modern designs. The lipstick-red sofa and ottoman were designed by Isamu Noguchi, as was the round table surrounded by Alvar Aalto lounge chairs. The floors are aluminum plate.

From his desk on the loft level, *and table were designed by*

Gardner faces the wall of *Charles Eames.*

windows. The molded chair

LEFT:

The glass counter in the bathroom appears to float on its glass-and-aluminum base. The bed is pushed up against the west wall of the apartment and the north-facing window so that Gardner can watch the sunrise above Lake Michigan.

BELOW:

Aluminum panels pivot to open the kitchen to the conversation room, with its wall of windows. Valerio designed the maple cabinets. Floors in the functional areas, including the kitchen, are terrazzo. Jamaica bar stools are from Knoll.

Attached to one of the aluminum panels, the media center pivots to face either the bed or the conversation area.

OPPOSITE:

With the aluminum panels open, Gardner can enjoy the view through the apartment's windows from his whirlpool bath.

HUGH NEWELL JACOBSEN

Abstracting the Vernacular
Welles Residence

LONG BEFORE REGIONALISM became an architectural fashion, Hugh Newell Jacobsen mastered the art of abstracting the vernacular. Whether he is designing in Greece or in Ohio, he creates buildings that fit comfortably into their surroundings. Yet by the clarity of its plan, the crispness of its modeling, and the exaltation of light and view, a Jacobsen house is distinctive and recognizable. He designs with a keen awareness of how a house will reveal itself to visitors. "The approach to a house," Jacobsen says, "should be a drum roll, and inside, that expectation must be fulfilled."

The Welles residence in northwest Ohio is a quintessential Jacobsen house. Driving along a road bordering the Maumee River through farmland, you might easily miss the entrance to the 8-acre property, which is marked only by a white mailbox and a double row of spruce trees. The long driveway curves down from a plateau. Once you break the crest of the hill, you catch a glimpse of the river and the building's tall white chimneys and vaults, which poke out above the evergreens planted on the public side of the site. At the end of the driveway, you face the front door. There are no win-

dows to reveal the interiors. The size and plan remain a mystery.

Inside, just to the left of the entrance, a dome-topped atrium spotlights the center of the house from which its four branches unfold. The light draws your eye to the left, toward the living room, where an arched wall of windows and sliding glass doors reveals the view of the river and a concrete bridge. At the beginning of the century, when it was built for the trolley line that connected Toledo with Lima, the bridge's 12 arches formed the longest concrete structure in the world. Time and nature have mellowed it to a golden ruin from which a tangle of trees and vines grow in a manner that, according to Jacobsen, "would have pleased Giovanni Piranesi."

Jacobsen was so taken with the romance of this view that he designed the house so that the bridge and river can be seen from every room. The main bar of the house's cruciform plan parallels the river. The shorter crossbar, rather than being set at a right angle, is skewed by 30 degrees and aimed toward the bridge. The longer bar contains three bedrooms and baths on one side of the atrium, balanced by the kitchen and garage on the other. The angle of the crossbar determined the parallelogram shape of rooms, a shape echoed in details such as built-in dresser drawers. The crossbar extends from the living room. Four steps lead you to the atrium under the 8-foot dome, and from there, through an archway to the library, which also serves as a dining room. The library shares the living room's view of the bridge and river through the clean sweep of light-filled space.

Arches in the ceiling and windows above the sliding glass doors echo the arches of the bridge. Though the house has so much glass, the Welleses have been pleasantly surprised by how much wall space Jacobsen

provided for their growing collection of art. He has, over the years, developed a detailed questionnaire to determine a family's needs before designing a living space. How many people will be seated for dinner? How much wall space is needed for art? How many linear feet for books? How much storage space for shoes? All of their functional requirements are woven seamlessly into his designs. His schematics come with a furniture plan, so his clients know how the rooms will work, and he often designs much of the furniture himself.

Typically, Jacobsen has "floated" the furniture, so the limits of the rooms are not defined, and he has used the same flooring (white travertine) inside and out, to merge the interiors with outdoor spaces. Details such as moldings, baseboards, and door frames are absent. Although some postmodern architecture aspires to a classical quality through decorative detailing, Georgia Welles points out that "Jacobsen's work is classical because of its symmetry and order. This discipline brings great serenity to his houses."

In the living room, an arched
wall of glass frames the view of
the bridge. Jacobsen designed the
rug, the Plexiglas table behind
the sofas, the benches, and the
coffee table. Symmetrical
fireplaces face one another. The
drawing above the fireplace on
the right is Bird by Dappled Sea
by Milton Avery; the painting
above the fireplace on the left is
Speedboat in Pale Sea *by the*
same artist. Ficus trees in the
living room are fed and watered
by concealed pipes.

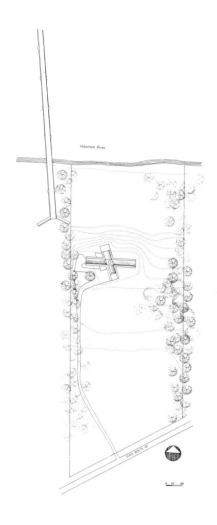

Site Plan

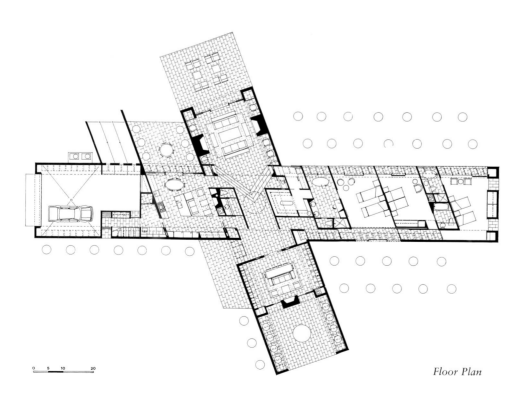

Light shines through the circular
dome at the center of the house
highlighting two large paintings:
on the right, Songs: Over the
Rainbow *by Kenneth Noland; on*
the left, Ocean Park No. 32 *by*
Richard Diebenkorn. V-shaped
steps lead to the living room.
Floors throughout the house and
on the outdoor terraces are
honed travertine.

Floor Plan

LEFT:

The placement of the French country oak table in the center of the room, surrounded by green velvet and brass stacking chairs, allows the library to serve as a dining room. The woodblock print highlighted above the fireplace is Ochre *by Diebenkorn.*

BELOW LEFT:

At night the sunny yellow print by Diebenkorn, on the far wall of the library, is visible from the terrace outside the living room.

RIGHT:

Jacobsen's trademark egg crate bookcases line two walls in the library. The table holds part of the owners' collection of duck and fish decoys.

Just up the steps from the living room, doors slide open to reveal a mirrored bar. The glass shelves hold part of the owners' collection of pre-Columbian ceramics.

A fireplace provides a cozy focus on one side of the kitchen. Above it hangs O.P. 84 #1 by Diebenkorn. The door to the side of the fireplace conceals a television.

Georgia Welles requested a large eat-in kitchen so that she would not have to keep asking her husband what was on the evening news while she was in the kitchen, preparing dinner. The dining table faces the view of the bridge through sliding glass doors. They open to a terrace that is enclosed on three sides. In warm weather the court is used for dining under the shade of pear and apple trees.

HUGH NEWELL JACOBSEN

. . . . .

Abstracting the Vernacular
Jacobsen Residence

JACOBSEN'S OWN HOUSE is located in the historic Georgetown section of Washington, D.C., just a few blocks from his office. According to records in the Georgetown Public Library, the house was originally built in the federal style in the early nineteenth century. In 1871, a third floor was added, and the facade made "tasteful" by the addition of an Italianate cornice and bay window. In keeping with the then-fashionable Italianate style it was painted the color of sandstone.

When Jacobsen remodeled the house in 1968, with his customary deference to a neighborhood, he left the facade almost intact. From the shady, brick-paved street, the house looks very much like its neighbors except for a discreet plaque on the door, which says "back door." The new main entry to the house is revealed only when you open the gate to an ivy-covered court bounded by the original house, a new wall that extends along the street, and the two-story addition that stretches behind the original house. Jacobsen "demoted" the front door to kitchen door, and removed the pediment trim, entry light, and address plate from the door on the street and placed them on the gate to the forecourt.

Inside, the house is vintage Jacobsen. From the forecourt, you enter at the center, where Jacobsen created an axis that extends the length of the enlarged house from the 1871 bay window, which he lowered to the floor in the dining room. This axis continues uninterrupted through the new living room, where a bay window reveals the garden. "The garden," Jacobsen says, "is the magic of a Georgetown house." A library adjacent to the living room shares the garden view. For his urban oasis, he created a stone terrace extending to a bank of ivy, which stretches toward the columnar American holly trees planted along the back garden wall. The trees are individually lit, so the garden can be seen from the house at night. This house was the first project in which Jacobsen employed his now-familiar floor-to-ceiling openings between rooms, without moldings or baseboards. Nothing interrupts the eye as it is drawn to the view of the garden.

To contain his family's ever-expanding collection of books, Jacobsen has, over time, added his trademark egg crate bookcases, first to the library and then to the dining room. Over the years, he has changed the furnishings, combining classic modern pieces, such as the Scarpa sofas in the living room and a Finnish Cognac chair in the study, with furniture of his own design, such as the prototype sofa and the coffee table in the study. These furnishings, plus a few remarkable antiques, such as the fifteenth-century dining table, have created a serene background for a growing collection of art, antiquities, and silver-framed family photos. The house, with time, grows increasingly personal.

Recently Jacobsen added three perfectly proportioned reproduction columns to the stair hall: a Doric column from the Temple of Poseidon, an Ionic column from the Temple of Artemis, and a composite column from a small house in Pompeii. While clearly contemporary in designing for the needs of families today, Jacobsen's inspiration is deeply rooted in classical architecture. Every morning when he comes downstairs, the columns remind him of a favorite quotation from his great mentor, Louis Kahn, with whom he studied at Yale: "The great moment in architecture—when the wall divided and the column became—took place in Greece."

In the living room, sliding glass
doors flank a floor-to-ceiling bay
window that looks out to the
garden. Sofas and armchairs

designed by Carlo Scarpa face
each other across a pair of steel-
and-glass Barcelona coffee tables
by Ludwig Mies van der Rohe.

Silver candlesticks on the coffee
table represent the three orders of
classical columns.

ABOVE:

An entire wall of the library is lined with Jacobsen's trademark egg crate bookcases. Jacobsen designed the sofa and the coffee table with a French marble top. Two chairs (designed by Charles Pollock) face one another across an Omega desk designed by Hans Eichenberger. The ottoman was designed by Ludwig Mies van der Rohe, the Cognac chair by Eero Saarinen. A variety of objects reflecting Jacobsen's extensive interests are displayed on the desk: a silver Shaker box, a tiny book of architectural stamps, a sculpture dating from the Middle Kingdom that he found when he was working in Cairo, a nineteenth-century Dutch staircase (a maquette that a cabinetmaker would execute to prove his abilities to an architect), a fragment of a sculpted head from Cambodia, a ribbon presented to a soldier who served in the Great War, and a tiny book containing some of the writings of Thomas Jefferson.

LEFT:

In the living room (looking toward the library) the painting on the left is by Josef Albers; on the right stands a perfectly scaled model of a portion of Ange-Jacque Gabriel's Hotel du Garde-meuble du Roi that Jacobsen found in a Parisian shop that sells architectural maquettes. The Roman terra-cotta head on the right coffee table dates from the eighteenth century.

Floor Plan

THIRD FLOOR

0 4 8 16

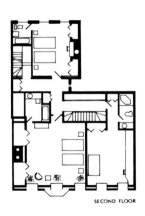

SECOND FLOOR

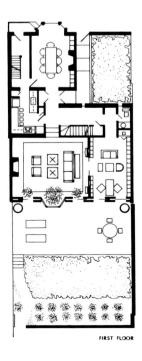

FIRST FLOOR

DARCY BONNER
& SCOTT HIMMEL

. . . .

Restoring Elegance
Bonner Residence

WHETHER DESIGNING a sleekly contemporary retail space, a traditional interior, or a sofa, "what matters to us is the opportunity to be inventive," Darcy Bonner says. Scott Himmel, who was his partner in the Chicago-based firm Himmel/Bonner, agrees: "It is boring to play music in just one key." It is essential to them both to create a complete environment. "One of the things I admire about Carlo Scarpa's work is that there was no difference between doing a building and doing a doorknob," Bonner says. Himmel elaborates: "Doing it all makes you better at each. If you can play in every key, you can really play."

Himmel and Bonner first met as undergraduates when they were studying architecture at Tulane University. They lost track of one another after graduation when Bonner returned to his native Dallas and Himmel to Chicago. Several years later, when Bonner had moved to Chicago, he ran into Himmel at an architectural licensing seminar. "I remembered Darcy as the best designer at Tulane when we were students there and therefore suggested that we work together," Himmel recalls.

Since becoming partners, they have led somewhat parallel lives: they married women from the same small town, and each of the two couples has three children of similar ages. Bonner and Himmel and their families lived for years in one of Mies van der Rohe's apartment towers on Lake Shore Drive in Chicago, an appropriate address for two young architects who admired the work of the early modernists.

Several years after they formed their architectural partnership, the firm was hired to renovate one of Chicago's grand old apartment buildings on Lake Shore Drive. The nine-story building had been built in the 1920s but was divided into smaller units in the 1960s. Only three of the original layouts remained. Two of the apartments shared an elevator and had similar plans. "Those apartments made us see what elegance really is," Bonner recalls. "We wanted to get away from 8 $1/2$-foot ceilings and steel-and-aluminum sash windows." The partners were enticed by the 10-foot ceilings, triple-hung windows, and generously proportioned rooms. In particular, they admired the enfilade of main rooms. With no hallways in between the living room, dining room, and library, the rooms, which are on an axis, become one majestic sweep of space when the pocket doors between them slide open.

Bonner bought one of the two apartments that had an unchanged layout. It still had its original walnut paneling. He restored the paneling and removed the marbleized vinyl that covered the wooden floors. The dining-room paneling had been painted. Since it would be difficult to restore it, Bonner decided to emphasize the contrast by painting its walls a rich cream that becomes a highlight between the walnut-paneled living room and library. To further accentuate the dark luster of the paneling in those rooms, he bleached the oak floors and painted the ceilings and trim the color of the dining room.

In the walnut-paneled foyer of the Bonner apartment, an early-nineteenth-century Italian table holds an antique Japanese basket, a contemporary sculpture by Jean Reindel, and antique silver candlesticks. The rug is Moroccan. A mirror in a hand-carved, late-nineteenth-century Spanish frame hangs above the table.

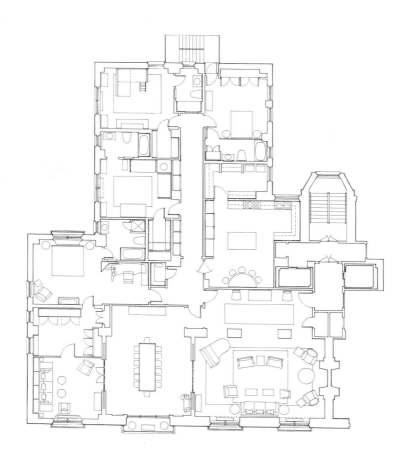

Floor Plan

The arched shape of the entry from the foyer to the living room is repeated in the windows' arched openings. In front of the fireplace, a generic flea-market table holds part of the Bonners' collection of Murano glass. The chairs to either side of the fireplace, upholstered in their original weathered leather, were found in a Parisian jewelry store. Above the fireplace, an English constructivist painting by Alistair Morton is displayed. On the mantle below the Morton is a bronze African sleeve ornament from the Kuba tribe. To the left is a grand tour model of the Temple of Castor. To the right of the fireplace are two collages by Gene Hedge.

In the dining room, Flea Market #31 dining chairs by Mattaliano, upholstered in leather the color of cream, surround an olive ash table, also by Mattaliano. The

Pierre Chareau–style bar cabinet on the right is a flea market find. The painting above the bar is by Gio Colucci. On the bar is part of a collection of primitive masks

and headdresses. The rug is a late-nineteenth-century Savonnerie.

The rug in the library is an eighteenth-century Aubusson. The sofa is the Colette three-seat sofa by Mattaliano. It is upholstered in a cotton chenille by Glant. On the table is an antique astrosphere. The vellum column table lamp is by Mattaliano.

ABOVE:

Bonner designed the aluminum lighting fixture in the dining room as a "vehicle to update the atmosphere. The low voltage bulbs," he explains, "throw punches of light in the room." The silver on the dining-room table is from the Paris flea market—except for the large bowl, which is actually the top of a tureen, a gift from Bonner's mother. On the left wall framing the study, a sculpture by Irving

Amen stands on a parchment-covered pedestal by Mattaliano. The painting at top left is by Robert Michel, a German constructivist; the one below is by Leo Prochownik, a German expressionist.

The table holding the tulips is an original by Jules Leleu. The sisal rug in the living room is from Stark; it is overlaid with a French eighteenth-century Aubusson. The club chairs, upholstered in suede, the color of cantaloupe, are Franc #1 by Mattaliano. The collage hanging on the living-room wall to the left of the dining room is by Bob Nichols. To the right, behind the piano, a painting by Francesco Monatti is displayed.

Bonner designed the sycamore

screens in the master bedroom.

The sheets are from Pratesi. The

bedside tables are attributed to

Donald Deskey.

In his living room, Himmel has
layered the stone-color carpet
with a French Aubusson rug and
eighteenth-century Indian zebra
skins. He replaced the apartment's overscaled fireplace
opening and mantel with a classic

nineteenth-century rouge
fireplace. In front of the fireplace
is an antique architectural
drawing. A Belgian art nouveau
table stands in front of one of the
living room's triple-hung
windows. The unlined curtains

are made of celadon-striped
taffeta. A seventeenth-century
tapestry covers the ottoman. The
white armchair was designed by
Jules Leleu. Across from it sits a
nineteenth-century reproduction
of an eighteenth-century French

chair; it is still upholstered in the
original fabric. The 1930s French
chair to the left of the fireplace
was a flea market find. Against
the wall to the left of the
fireplace stands a French faux
tortoise secretary from the 1930s.

DARCY BONNER
& SCOTT HIMMEL

· · · · ·

Restoring Elegance
Himmel Residence

THE APARTMENT ACROSS THE HALL from Bonner's had been owned by a prominent Chicago family for over 50 years. "The notion that it had a history" appealed to Himmel, a native Chicagoan. Moreover, not many buildings in Chicago have such dramatic layouts. He, too, was seduced by the sweeping space, and soon he was living across the hall from his partner.

Himmel's apartment had at one time been renovated, so he added detailing and finishes discreetly, to make it seem as though they had always been there. He added about 40 percent of the moldings, glazed the walls, and redid the fireplace. "The building design is French, but the mantel was Midwest hocum, too high and too wide," Himmel says. He replaced it with a classic nineteenth-century French rouge fireplace. He remodeled the kitchen and master bath, but he left the apartment's plan basically intact, with the exception of taking space away from the rectangular dining room to create a closet. The result is a square 18-by-18-foot room, the perfect frame for a large round table and a spectacular nineteenth-century Venetian glass chandelier that Himmel had his eye on for some time. When he bought the apartment, he knew that he at last had a home for the chandelier, which inspired the color scheme of the main rooms. The colors deepen in a subtle progression from the vanilla and celadons with gilded gray-green moldings in the living room to the old vellum in the dining room, culminating with olive green in the library.

Since the early 1980s, Himmel and Bonner had become habitues of Paris flea markets, buying furniture for themselves and for clients. There they discovered the furniture designed by Jean-Michel Frank and his circle. They found the early French modernists' combination of simplicity of line and sumptuous finishes enormously appealing. However, the authentic furniture of the period became difficult to find, and available reproductions seemed "off." Working with the Welles Furniture Company, a third-generation, family-owned establishment that had been manufacturing custom-designed furniture for architects since the time of Ludwig Mies van der Rohe, Himmel and Bonner began reproducing some of the French moderne pieces they admired. When the company closed, Himmel/Bonner took it over, changing the name to Mattaliano in honor of its founder. They manufacture a line of furniture meticulously reproduced from the French moderne classics. (Himmel and Bonner continue to share office space, but now run two separate firms.)

Although neither of the two families' apartments resembles a laboratory, they are both places of experimentation. Bonner and Himmel often try out the Mattaliano designs in their own homes. Furnishings and objects are constantly changing. A collection of Samurai armor is sold and is replaced with primitive masks; a client buys a classic French moderne chair and in its place appears one of the Mattaliano reproductions. "The places I live in are always the best training ground," Himmel says. "You don't really understand something until you live with it."

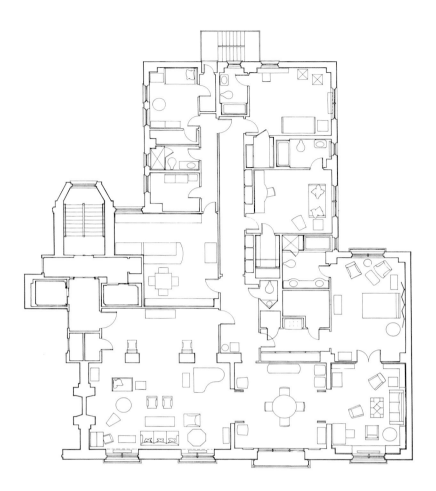

Floor Plan

The library has mirrored paneled doors that open to the master bedroom. The room is lined with grille-front bookshelves. The Mattaliano sofa is based on a 1920s design by Jacques-Emile Ruhlmann. It is upholstered in a quilted ecru fabric with pillows covered in an African tribal cloth. Another zebra skin stretches beneath the Frank vellum coffee table. The Flea Market #1 club chair, also a Mattaliano reproduction, is upholstered in sueded leather.

A Lyon & Healy baby grand piano stands in one corner of the living room. On the other side of the opening to the dining room is an Italian futurist bar from Turin made of Makassar ebony; above it hangs a 1923 painting by Leo Prochownik, whom Himmel describes as "a second-tier German expressionist." The Colette sofa from Mattaliano is upholstered in a Brunschwig & Fils chenille. The matching club chair is also from Mattaliano. Himmel designed the coffee table from Indiana limestone. The pull-up chairs upholstered with an animal skin are, Himmel thinks, an Italian design from the 1940s.

OPPOSITE:

A 24-spoke nineteenth-century Venetian glass chandelier is the centerpiece of the dining room. A fabric from Pierre Frey, inspired by an African design, is spread on the round dining table. Beneath it lies a paisley fabric from Old World Weavers. The cream-colored oak dining chairs are by Jean-Michel Frank. To the right is a 1930s German cabinet by Soulek. Above it hangs a cubist drawing from the flea market.

RIGHT:

The master bath was completely remodeled by Himmel. The walls are covered in Italian white marble. The black Portuguese marble vanity top, supported by a polished chrome frame, holds two sinks.

The Himmel's oldest child, Alexander, has toy towers designed by his father. On the floor is one of Alexander's Lego creations. The vinyl floor's checkerboard pattern is edged with a contrasting border.

Himmel, who serves as the family chef, completely remodeled the kitchen. The eat-in kitchen has a floor of black and white ceramic tile, which also is used for the sides of the granite topped island. Shiny copper pots hang from a rack in easy reach of the work island. Frosted-glass cabinet doors are framed in cerused oak.

CHARLES GWATHMEY

. . . .

Mellowing Modernism

FROM THE NOW-FAMOUS HOUSE and studio he designed for his parents in 1966 to the apartment he presently shares with his wife, Charles Gwathmey's architecture is often described as sculptural—no gesture is wasted, and every line has meaning. Gwathmey studied architecture at the University of Pennsylvania when Louis Kahn was teaching there and completed his studies at Yale with Paul Rudolph. However, it was probably the work of the early modernists that had the greatest impact on his work. Early in his career Gwathmey, with Michael Graves, became one of the New York Five, whose work at the time recalled early modernism. Eventually the five architects went in different directions, but Gwathmey remained true to modernism.

The house and studio on eastern Long Island that Gwathmey, at the age of 27, designed for his artist parents brought him immediate fame and launched his career. The two small buildings, which became much-imitated icons on the Long Island landscape, have the strong, logical geometry and sculptural form of Le Corbusier's villas, but instead of stucco, Gwathmey used the quintessential American building material: wood.

In 1968, after a three-year stint in the office of Edward Larrabee Barnes, Gwathmey formed a partnership with Robert Siegel. Their firm became known for spare, elegant houses and interiors in the modernist tradition. Over the years the work has evolved beyond that of the original modernists. As the requirements of their projects become more complex, the geometry and the palette of materials and color grew more sumptuous. So the now-familiar labeling of Gwathmey as an American Le Corbusier has, in Gwathmey's own words, become "too literal and too easy."

Gwathmey has always had what he describes as a "holistic" approach to the design of houses. The furnishings and landscaping are always intrinsic to the design. Both the evolution of Gwathmey's design sensibility and his holistic approach are apparent in the apartment he designed for himself and his wife, Bette-Ann. The design succeeds in being at once abstract, complex, and sensual. "Designing for yourself presents an opportunity to experiment, and Bette-Ann is a good critic," Gwathmey says. After many years of living in a large family apartment in the same building, they were ready for a change. They wanted a loft but liked the amenities of the Fifth Avenue building and its majestic view of the Central Park Reservoir and the surrounding cityscape. So they bought a smaller apartment in the same building, and by completely gutting it—leaving only the perimeter walls and window openings—they achieved the freedom of a loft space.

Gwathmey always designs buildings with an acute awareness of the site, so the apartment's tenth-floor view of the reservoir directed the design. "I accepted the window openings as given and then made the usable spaces axial to them, but manipulated the sequence as an asymmetrical counterpoint," he says. An entry gallery leads into the apartment. The master bedroom and two baths open off the gallery on the right. At the end of the hallway to the left are the dining room, study, kitchen, and guest room and bath. A line carved into the ceiling curves from the gallery to the right drawing you into the living room and almost inevitably toward the view of the reservoir through the windows. A corner window facing south looks down on Fifth Avenue.

The floors reinforce the scheme. Maple flooring in 5 1/2-inch planks runs parallel and orthogonal to the building's perimeters, helping to define the rooms. Marble insets in the floor echo the curve of the dropped ceiling, articulating the circulation toward the view. This sequence is so skillfully handled that from the front door you seem to be pulled almost magnetically toward the view from the living-room wall of windows facing Fifth Avenue. Art and furnishings collected by Gwathmey since his student days are combined with

many of his own designs—the coffee tables, sofas, the entertainment unit that separates the living area from the library, the bed, all the cabinets, the dining-room table, even the dishes.

Characteristically, Gwathmey approached this interior design sculpturally, building out the walls in order to carve into them for the window openings and the fireplace. Even the ceiling is sculpted. "By making the walls appear thicker, you add to the sense of enclosure," he explains. "You really are inside a sculpture.

You cannot be in this apartment without looking up." These geometric forms, the curve of the ceiling, and the window and fireplace openings possess great drama, but because they have meaning and every detail is resolved, the apartment radiates great serenity. Bette-Ann Gwathmey describes their apartment as "a retreat within the city. You are surrounded by the view. It is at once serene, romantic, and exciting." At night, when the park and reservoir are lost in darkness and you are surrounded by the city's glittering lights, it is magical.

The view from the library looking toward the living room shows the entertainment unit Gwathmey designed to store stereo equipment. The fireplace appears to be carved into the living room wall.

Above the fireplace is a cast from a frieze designed by Louis Sullivan for the Garrick Theater. A rug designed by Josef Hoffman lies in front of the fireplace. To either side is Le Corbusier

seating, signed pieces Gwathmey bought in Zurich when he was a Fulbright scholar living in Europe. The clock on the right is late-nineteenth-century Viennese secessionist.

The gallery leading from the front door to the living room is lined on the left wall with Josef Albers's Homage to the Square series and on the right with a collection of black-and-white photographs. The bench and the mirrored screen were designed by Josef Hoffman. Next to the Hoffman screen is a set of Japanese early-twentieth-century Kabuki armor. The end of the gallery is punctuated by a column, and the dropped ceiling curves into the living room. The door on the right opens into the master bedroom.

Floor Plan

Gwathmey says he designed the entertainment unit to show that he could do a deconstructivist design. "It is my homage to Peter Eisenman," he says, with tongue in cheek. The unit is made from beech, ebony, stainless steel, and lacquer. The painting above the leather sofa is by the architect's father, Robert Gwathmey.

In the dining room, Hoffman chairs, which were Thonet prototypes, surround a table designed by Gwathmey. The lighting fixture was designed by Andreé Putman. When an addition to the Jewish Museum located across the street blocked the view, Gwathmey covered the windows that were on the right wall of the dining room. He created a clerestory of glass brick to bring in daylight. On the dining table are Gwathmey Siegel's candlesticks and bowl, designed for Swid Powell.

Gwathmey designed the counter stools as well as all of the kitchen cabinetry, which is made of cherry.

Gwathmey created a vaulted ceiling in the bedroom. The bed, covered by an Amish quilt, is his design. A painting by his father, Robert Gwathmey, hangs between the bedroom's two windows, which overlook the Central Park Reservoir. The rocking chair is a Thonet prototype.

The bedroom cabinetry was designed by Gwathmey in bird's-eye and solid maple. The door on the left leads to Gwathmey's bathroom, which faces his wife's on the other side of the room.

RIGHT:

Both master baths have windows overlooking the reservoir. The bathroom sink is placed in front of the window. A glass panel with an oval mirror slides in front of the window. When the panel slides away from the window, it serves as a front for the medicine and toiletries cabinet. The cabinetry is made of bird's-eye maple; the counter is onyx.

CHARLES MOORE
& ARTHUR ANDERSSON

. . . .

Collaborating with Joy
Moore Residence

WE HAD THE GOOD FORTUNE of visiting Charles Moore and photographing his house in Austin, Texas, just months before he died. Although his health was failing, it was so like him not to turn down a request for help and enlightenment, even at that time. The house is now being preserved as a historic site and architectural study center.

During the course of his amazingly fruitful and peripatetic career, Charles Moore held professorships at the University of California at Berkeley, Yale University, the University of California at Los Angeles, and the University of Texas at Austin. At each place he established a collaborative architecture office and designed a house for himself, sometimes more than one. The first 20 years of his practice were devoted primarily to the design of private residences. Since then he collaborated on the design of libraries, museums, and housing developments, but his fascination with houses remained constant.

The Place of Houses, his landmark book published in 1974 and written in collaboration with Gerald Allen and Donlyn Lyndon, says:

> *The failure of our surroundings to establish where and who we are seems to us to require a search for the habitable—both the physically habitable, where we can be comfortable and live our lives, and the metaphorically habitable, where we can go beyond where we actually are to wherever our imaginations will transport us. Establishing a territory for habitation, physical and metaphorical, is the prime basis of architecture.*

In his personal quest for "habitation," Moore designed eight houses for himself, including this compound in Austin, Texas. He was lured to Texas not only by a

tenured professorship but also by envisioning the "spread" he would create for himself there. But "spreads" were elusive and he finally settled on a gentle sloping acre of property shaded by Spanish and post oaks close to town. Its location is pleasant. The original house on it was not. Moore described it as "a rather nasty wood-floor cottage of 1936, that had been enlarged in 1950 by an even nastier addition on concrete slab."

The "spread" he created from this unpromising beginning is in many ways representative of his work. Like the majority of both his written and built projects, the Austin compound was the result of a collaborative effort. Richard Dodge and Arthur Andersson worked with Moore on the design. They decided that they would remodel the existing house for Moore and build a studio and a smaller house for Andersson, who had assisted Moore with the building of the 1984 New Orleans World's Fair and had moved to Austin to manage Moore's new office.

Moore's projects have been enriched by his remarkable recall of both architectural history and the places he has visited. In Austin, the idea for grouping the buildings around a courtyard with a swimming pool in the center was inspired by his memory of a long, raised tank at Geoffrey Bawa's office in Colombo, Sri Lanka. The entrance to the courtyard was derived from an old photograph of a wagon entrance to the Sherwood Ranch in Salinas, California. Despite these far-reaching allusions, the project was also grounded in a specific sense of place. The cluster of shed-roofed structures—three buildings linked by covered pergolas—that surround a central court recall the board-and-batten farmhouses of the nearby Texas hill country. Moreover, Moore said, awful as he thought it was, he

felt "a kind of archaeologist's morality about the existing house." He described the remodeling as "selective erasure." He left most of the windows intact, adding one large one. A pitched roof was raised over the original flat roof, and the ceiling and most interior walls were removed to reorder the interior space.

Moore wrote in an essay entitled "The Yin, the Yang and the Three Bears," that what all the houses he designed for himself "have in common (beside their modesty, and my residing in them) is a grand gesture, and since there was no client to offend but myself, they gave eight special chances to walk the thin edge of disaster." According to Andersson, Moore's big gestures "shape a space like environmental art." Texas required an especially big gesture, one that would include Moore's house, the court, the studio, and Andersson's house. The gesture in Austin is an ellipse that extends through Moore's house as a curved wall and is completed across the court with the fireplace wall of Andersson's house.

The foreword to *The Place of Houses* advises that to create a house of great worth, "you bind together the

goods and trappings of your life with your dreams to make a place that is uniquely your own." Moore's houses are distinguished by the joy with which he carried out those words. He traveled extensively and collected objects typically of little monetary value. In Austin, when visitors step inside the Viennese front door (found in a local architectural fragments shop), they see that Moore has bound together the "goods and trappings" of his life with the panache of a maestro. In the entry corridor, miniature Italian villages sit across from Mexican birdcages beneath shelves that hold toys and objects from several continents. The curve of the ellipse extends through the entry hall, swings around to provide a partition between the dining area and the kitchen, and continues as the fireplace wall in the living room. This strong geometric gesture orders a baroque, intensely polychromed pattern of objects: shields, books, toys, sculpture, and birdcages inhabited by ceramic painted birds. These objects are merrily set against walls painted with vibrant blues and corals. These colors were inspired by the oriental rug, which lies between the leather sofas in the living room.

Moore found the English dining table in an antique shop in Los Angeles. "Gazing down on the scene," he said, "is my great-great-grandmother." A Spanish chandelier hangs above the dining-room table. Simple wicker chairs at the table contrast with the chairs made of horns and cowhides around a small table in front of the kitchen. Moore found these chairs in Castroville, Texas. Along the wall that Moore says "ventures into my house along the planned oval" are painted shields designed by students in one of his architecture studios. Each one has a big kachina in the middle and a mask overhead; most of them are from Mexico.

This view of the entry looks toward the carved-wood Viennese front door. Along the window seat are Mexican birdcages inhabited by painted ceramic birds. The shelf above holds toys and objects collected by Moore in China, Chile, and Great Britain.

Across from the windows, in between pilasters, are bookshelves and Plexiglas boxes that contain miniature Italian villages and collections of bronze buildings.

Moore painted the original fireplace and decorated it with tile. "The mantelpiece," he said, "inhabited by an assortment of angels, was made by Arthur Andersson out of cheap museum board. After getting the shapes and forms we desired, we intended to render them in plywood. Even though I am pleased with the way the palm trees look, this has not happened yet." Two leather sofas face one another across a large coffee table. Beneath its glass top is a painted lake scene with a little village populated with ducks, turtles, and toy soldiers. A lamp made from an old glass jug sits on a painted red chest that Moore brought back from China.

Just across from the fireplace, three steps up from the living room, is a sitting area drenched with sunshine from the largest window in the house. From there more steps lead to a sleeping loft. The Adirondack chair was designed by Moore. He explained that he "updated the classic with my own shapes, wide armrests, and a soft purple coat of paint with orange and red patterns near the top." Shelves near the top of the room hold part of his enormous collection of wooden animals. Most of them originate from Central and South America.

OPPOSITE:

The design for the gate to the compound was inspired by a photograph by Roger Sturtevant of a wagon entrance to the Sherwood Ranch in Salinas, California. Andersson designed the mirror framed in tin and painted wood as a birthday surprise for Charles Moore in 1992. It hangs above the entry gate. Steps lead down to the court, which is bisected by a lap pool.

Moore painted the original concrete floor with a pattern of circles within squares, covered with several coats of acrylic to make it shine. This detail shows the floor in the entry corridor.

Just inside the front door, a flight of Cape Cod steps leads up to the attic bedroom and study. Windows open one side of the entry corridor to the view of the court. Colorful pillows on top of a low bookcase form a long window bench.

CHARLES MOORE
& ARTHUR ANDERSSON

. . . .

Collaborating with Joy
Andersson Residence

ALTHOUGH THE EXTERIOR DESIGN of Andersson's house is similar to Moore's house, the similarity ends when you step inside the door. "I would not be comfortable living with the level of intensity in Charles's house," Andersson says. For so young an architect (Andersson was only 25 at the time he designed the house) he maintained an extraordinary discipline. He was determined not to overload the 770-square-foot house, which he describes as a "24-by-36-foot trailer with high ceilings." Instead he limited himself to a few bold strokes that enliven and enhance the small space.

He partitioned the long room with a freestanding Styrofoam wall that is open from waist height to a thick, richly carved lintel topped by an oculus. It divides the room into living and study/dining areas without a complete visual interruption. The exaggerated scale of the wall seems to enlarge the space, an idea Andersson credits to Donato Bramante, the Italian Renaissance architect who would aggrandize a relatively small chapel with an overscaled canopy. The door to the cloister at San Carlo alle Quattro Fontane by Francesco Borromini in Rome also was an inspiration. "The thickness of things disappeared with the modern movement," Andersson says. "The classical idiom has withstood the test of time, but it is not just about pediments and arches, and it does not have energy when it is thoughtlessly reproduced."

Andersson ordered the long room with a cadence of windows on one side. On the other side an arched wall completes the oval of the wall in Moore's house. The shelves on this wall, he says, were inspired by the cliff dwellings of the hill towns along the Ganges River in India. This thick wall, which holds his extensive library, is penetrated by openings to the kitchen and bedroom. Andersson placed an eighteenth-century Irish Georgian door at the opening to the bedroom. He explains that because people were smaller then, the portal is only 6 feet 3 inches high. Here again, he has visually enlarged the space by playing with the scale—seen from across the room, the doorway seems more distant because it is smaller than usual.

The small house is very serene, mostly white and beige with color coming from the wall of books and a softly patterned geometric design painted on the floor. Although his interior may seem Spartan in comparison to Moore's, Andersson has introduced his characteristic wry humor into the house. Wall brackets above the bookcases hold black-and-white cutouts of photographs of great men from Texas history. While definitely his own man, Andersson has, like his mentor Charles Moore, enhanced his surroundings with joy.

Arthur Andersson's room divider, set on the diagonal and topped by a Styrofoam entablature, frames the door to the bedroom as seen from the living area. Just behind the room divider is a

Mexican table that serves as a desk and dining table. The fireplace (stove) is manufactured by Rais-Wittus. The two 1920s chairs that sit in front of the room divider were found in

London. Giovanni Nolli's plan of Rome, which Andersson mounted on foam core, is on the far wall. He hand-painted the canvas curtains. Andersson has combined classical vocabulary

with a bit of local lore by placing cutouts of black-and-white photographs of Texan heroes on brackets above the bookcases.

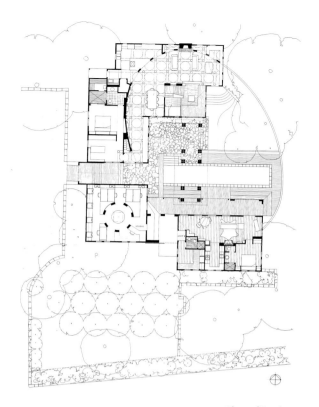

Plan of Studio

Antique brackets from Barcelona

are mounted to the heraldic arch

on the side facing the table.

Andersson paneled his bathroom

walls with standing-seam tin. The

glass door on the left opens to

the shower, the door on the right

to the toilet.

An eighteenth-century Irish door that Andersson found in Dallas opens to the bedroom. On the left is an Indian shutter from Delhi.

Venetian blinds control the light from tall windows behind the bed, which is covered with a simple white blanket.

FREDERIC SCHWARTZ

· · · · · · ·

Fusing Color and Pattern

THE MOMENT YOU STEP INTO the foyer of this Manhattan apartment, you know you have entered a place different from any other that you have experienced. Dubbed "the Hall of the Giant Rose" by its designer, Frederic Schwartz, a partner in Anderson/Schwartz Architects in New York City, the foyer sets the tone for the rest of the apartment. The chairs that line its walls hint at the major collection of twentieth-century furniture that fills the spacious rooms overlooking Central Park. The stenciled background of overscaled flowers refers to the apartment's view of Central Park and the patterns of furniture and objects in the collection. The Hall of the Giant Rose is a prelude to the conversation that Schwartz has developed between this collection of twentieth-century furniture and decorative arts and the architecture of the apartment.

The owner, Andrew Cogan, senior vice president of marketing for Knoll International, had an early introduction to twentieth-century design. He is the son of Marshall Cogan, who was the chairman and chief executive officer of Knoll. At the age of 15, Andrew Cogan bought a chair designed by Charles Eames. His collection now includes twentieth-century classics by modern masters such as Frank Lloyd Wright, Marcel Breuer, Gerrit Rietveld, Charles Eames, Alvar Aalto, Ettore Sottsass, Isamu Noguchi, Ludwig Mies van der Rohe, Robert Venturi, and Frank Gehry, as well as carpets, furniture, and lighting fixtures custom-designed for the apartment by Schwartz.

Cogan and Schwartz met when Schwartz was the project director on Knoll's collection of Venturi chairs. The "Grandmother" pattern on some of the prototype Knoll chairs in Cogan's collection was adapted by Robert Venturi from a tablecloth owned by Schwartz's grandmother. Schwartz counts Venturi, along with Joseph Esherick, Denise Scott Brown, and Alan Buchsbaum, as his great mentors. Schwartz was the first in what has become a tradition of young apprentices

who live in Venturi and Scott Brown's house while working for them. He went on to become an associate of the firm and then to head their New York office. In addition to their independent projects, Schwartz and his partner, Ross Anderson, are collaborating with Venturi and Scott Brown on the design for the Staten Island Ferry Terminal and a capitol building in southwest France.

Many architects, confronted with a collection of furniture and decorative arts that extends from the Bauhaus to postmodernism, from De Stijl to Memphis, might have opted to place this museum-quality collection in a gallerylike setting of unadorned white walls with track lighting, to spotlight the objects. Schwartz, however, points out that: "A good designer must see things other don't see and combine things others would not combine." He set about orchestrating a retinue of craftspeople and artisans to create a setting for the collection that would vibrate with color and pattern.

He first completed a renovation of the rooms, restoring and, when necessary, re-creating moldings, mantels, and cornices to reinforce the apartment's traditional quality. To create an eat-in kitchen, a practical solution for Cogan's on-the-run life, Schwartz combined several small maids' rooms with the existing kitchen. With the addition of an adjacent apartment that had fortuitously become available, several years after Cogan moved into the prewar building, the entrance hall was doubled in size, and a separate dining room and a sitting room were added. For the most part, Schwartz retained the apartment's traditional layout and room proportions. However, he eliminated the doors between the more public rooms to provide a glimpse of the collection in adjoining rooms and a visual layering of colors and patterns.

Thus from the living room you can see the giant roses stenciled in the hall, as well as the patterns of the leaded-glass doors Schwartz designed to separate the

living room from the master bedroom. The colors and patterns in the doors refer to the work of both Wright and Sottsass. Just down the hall from the master bedroom is the library, with stenciling inspired by both Mondrian and Rietveld.

Poetic passages from Italo Calvino's book *Invisible Cities*, which Cogan and Schwartz faxed to one another during the course of the renovation, are reproduced in red paint on the walls of the living room and eat-in kitchen. By an almost magical serendipity, after Schwartz had designed a rug for the living room that abstracts the plan of Manhattan, they found a passage in the book about a carpet that with pattern and color represents a city: "Every inhabitant of Eudoxia compares the carpet's immobile order with his own image of the city, an anguish of his own, and each can find, concealed among the arabesques, an answer, the story of his life, the twists of fate." These words, reproduced on one of the living room's walls, form a striking background for the rug Schwartz designed.

Just as each of the cities described in Calvino's book has its own story, so do Schwartz's projects. At the same time he was working on this apartment, he designed a loft that is "sleek and modern, all black and white. I do not believe that there is only one acceptable style," he says. "There are all kinds of people and all kinds of places, and it makes an architect richer to experience working in a variety of ways."

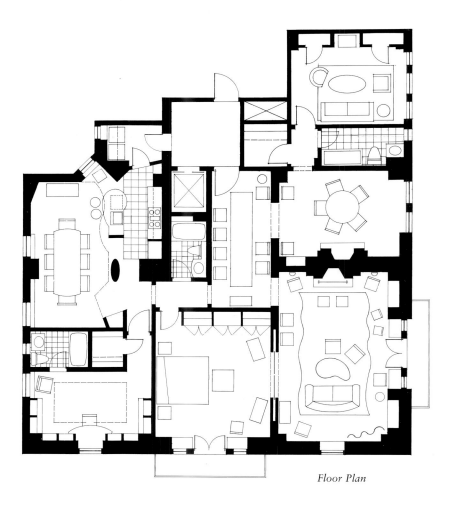

Floor Plan

Just inside the front door, visitors are greeted by the Hall of the Giant Rose. The stenciled walls, designed by Schwartz and painted by Braby & Strackbein, form a lively background for part of the owner's major collection of classic twentieth-century chairs. The chairs in the foyer, clockwise from left: chair and stool designed by Wright for the Trier house; c. 1950 prototype painted tubular chair by Mies van der Rohe at a table designed by Gehry; wooden lounge chair designed by Eames in 1946; two chairs designed by Venturi in 1984 for Knoll International; chair designed by Gehry, called High Sticking. The wall sconces by Venturi and the rug by Schwartz were custom-designed for the apartment when the foyer was enlarged.

In the living room, light from the windows that overlook Central Park pours across the rug Schwartz designed to abstract the plan of Manhattan and celebrate the park; it is called New York, New York and was fabricated by V'Soske. Furnishings by modern masters include a glass coffee table with wood base by Noguchi; chairs below a quotation from Calvino's Invisible Cities were both designed by Rietveld; the chair to the left of the fireplace was designed by Wright. Gehry's Experimental Armchair stands to the right of the fireplace. The light sconce designed by Schwartz was fabricated by (Art + Light) Lehr Company.

At first sight nothing seems to resemble Eudoxia less than the design of that carpet, laid out in symmetrical motives whose patterns are repeated along straight and circular lines, interwoven with brilliantly colored spires, in a repetition that can be followed throughout the whole woof. But if you can pause and examine it carefully, you become convinced that each place in the carpet corresponds to a place in the city and all the things contained in the city are included in the design, arranged according to their true relationship, which escapes your eye distracted by the bustle, the throngs, the shoving. All of Eudoxia's confusion, the mules' braying, the lamp[...] smell is what is evident in the ind[...] but the carpet pro[...] you grasp; the city shows its [...]int from which scheme implicit in [...]e geometrical [...]ail.

It is easy to get lo[...] [...]hen you concentrate and s[...] [...]u recognize the street you were seeking in a crimson or indigo or magenta thread which, in a wide loop, brings you to the purple enclosure that is your real destination. Every inhabitant of Eudoxia compares the carpet's immobile order with his own image of the city, an anguish of his own, and each can find, concealed among the arabesques, an answer, the story of his life, the twists of fate.

Italo Calvino, *Invisible Cities*, pg. 96

A fire screen, called Symbols of the Universe, with His and Hers andirons designed by Schwartz and fabricated by Solebury Forge, contrast with the original fireplace mantel that was restored and painted white. On the mantel, a model of a Rietveld chair stands next to a painting by Joan Nelson.

Schwartz designed leaded-glass doors in patterns inspired by Wright and Sottsass to separate the master bedroom from the living room. The doors, named Right and Wrong, were fabricated by Nancy Howell Studio. The vibrant colors are echoed in the Rolling Thunder multicore rolling television stand designed by Schwartz and fabricated by A. Leinoff Woodworking. The red rocking chair is by Eames. On the classic steel-and-glass coffee table by Florence Knoll is a Memphis vase designed by Marco Zanini.

In the eat-in kitchen, chairs designed by Venturi and a tubular metal chair by Mies van der Rohe encircle the Point and Slab dining table designed by Schwartz and fabricated by A. Leinoff Woodworking. The Skyscraper chair, also called the Liberty chair, designed by Schwartz and fabricated by Tansunya, presides in a corner next to glass shelves.

Venturi designed the side table. Food for thought and conversation is provided by a cornice of red letters spelling out the quotation from Calvino's Invisible Cities. "Cities, like dreams, are made of desires and fears, even if the thread of their discourse is secret, their rules are absurd, their perspectives deceitful, and everything conceals something else."

The sitting room's bold color scheme was inspired by Linkage, a painting by Bruce Robbins. The rug, called Pencil Points, was fabricated by V'Soske and designed by Alan Buchsbaum. The bright yellow daybed, designed by Jasper Morris, has

pillows covered in fabric by Salvador Dali. The black chair on the left was designed by Aalto, and the plywood chair on the right by Gehry; the coffee table is by Eames.

The new dining room has a view of Central Park on one side and opens to the Hall of the Giant Rose on the other. Venturi's chairs, in "Grandmother" and "Paola Navona" patterns,

surround the round dining table, also designed by Venturi. The apartment's original wooden fireplace was stripped and restored to the natural wood.

GISUE HARIRI & MOJGAN HARIRI

· · · · · · ·

Pushing the Edge

THE PUBLICATION of the striking steel staircase in this loft launched Hariri & Hariri into the limelight of New York City's avant-garde design scene. A handsomely crafted, ingenious solution to a complex problem, the staircase remains representative of the firm's work.

"The excitement is in pushing the edge," says Gisue Hariri, who with her sister Mojgan started their own New York City–based architectural firm in 1986, just three years after they completed their studies at Cornell. The Iranian-born sisters came to the United States to study architecture, but the buildings and designs of their homeland have remained an influence. The interest in contrasting materials, site-oriented buildings that work well in the harsh climate of southern Iran, and the tradition of craftsmanship are all memories the sisters carry with them and convey in their designs.

When in 1987 Kathleen Schneider asked Hariri & Hariri to renovate a duplex, penthouse loft she had bought in one of the late-nineteenth-century cast-iron buildings found in New York City's SoHo neighborhood, the young architects had almost no built projects to show her. She decided to hire them anyway. They came highly recommended by friends in Manhattan's design community, and Schneider, who is the director of the Children's Museum in SoHo and an artist herself, says she "liked their energy." She does not regret her decision. "The loft is both livable and artistic," she says. "It is a comfort to come home."

When the Hariris took on the design, the space had already been partially renovated. The high ceilings and large open spaces typical of the cast-iron buildings of this formerly industrial district remained. "Our intention was to keep the character of the existing loft while transforming it to develop a habitable space for our client," Mojgan Hariri explains. To satisfy Schneider's request for an open space suitable for infor-

mal entertaining, and with sufficient wall space to display her art collection, they kept the lower floor fairly open: organizing the space around two parallel walls—the fireplace wall and a freestanding plaster wall with two oversized steel-and-glass doors, that divides the living room from a study. The architects left the existing kitchen in place and designed a bar that partially screens the workspace and provides an attractive focal point for the living room. The solution for this floor was straightforward and immediately apparent, but the resolution of the vertical circulation in the loft posed a challenge.

Schneider was determined to have her bedroom on the top floor "up among the clouds," and the architects realized that it would be necessary to replace the existing spiral staircase that, due to the number of its rotations and open grating, vibrated to a frightening degree. Since there was almost no room to spare if the architects were to create a bedroom and bath on that second level, they were not able to expand the existing 5-by-5-foot opening in the ceiling to accommodate a larger staircase. "After many attempts," Gisue explains, "we came up with a hybrid stair, partially straight and partially spiral. The two stairs are structurally independent but joined by a single sheet of steel, curving in a logarithmic spiral." It was welded and molded on the site by artists Dan George and Mark Gibian. Welding the steel eliminated the need for bolts and provided a continuous, sculptural surface. Moving up and down the staircase, one is simultaneously inside and outside the single sheet of cold-rolled steel. The stair railings end in a circular pattern of rings that the architects also used in the design of the pendant light fixtures and bar stools, produced by sculptor Scott R. Madison.

The color blue, which Schneider loves, unifies the design. The color appears in the marble counter and on the wooden floors, stained in light blue-gray. Deep blue covers the library walls; the doors are stained steel-blue; soft blue appears on the walls of the master bedroom. In the spring, when the wisteria planted on the cedar wood trellis in the roof garden blooms, it forms a buoyant blue canopy. A spiral stair leads to a private sun deck beneath the blue sky.

The Hariris often design lighting and furnishings for the interiors of their projects, and some of these designs are being manufactured and are available through George Kovacs. Their work has increasingly gained recognition for its use of tough materials such as steel, aluminum, wire mesh, and sandblasted glass in unusual and poetic ways. "I hope we never get too comfortable with a known material or design element," Gisue says. They continue to push the edge.

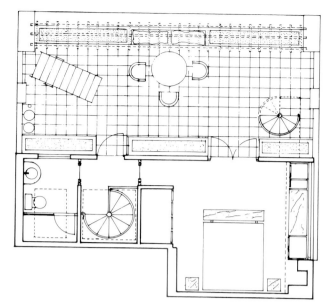

Upper Floor Plan

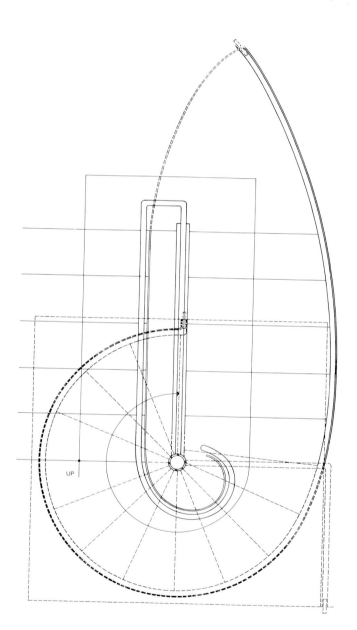

Stair Drawing

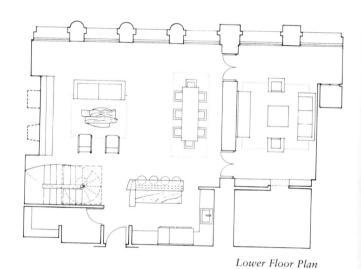

Lower Floor Plan

The loft's brilliant staircase was designed by the Hariris and was welded and molded on site by sculptors Mark Gibian and Dan George. The bar stools and pendant light fixtures, produced by sculptor Scott R. Madison, were designed by the architects to echo the pattern of rings at the ends of the staircase railing.

In a masterly juxtaposition of
materials, the architects had the
fireplace wall treated with hand-
troweled stucco to produce a

rough texture accented by a linear
marble mantel and a punched-in
log box.

The kitchen bar, with a blue marble counter and

mahogany and brushed-steel support, illustrates the

Hariris' ability to juxtapose materials in handsome

and unexpected designs.

Steel-framed glass doors designed
by the architects lead from the
master bedroom to the roof
garden. The heating unit to the
left of the doors was imported
from Switzerland.

The architects framed the roof
garden with a rose arbor and
wisteria trellis made of cedar-
wood.

The mirror, the steel-framed,
sandblasted glass window, and
the vanity with blue marble
countertop in the master
bathroom were all designed by
Hariri & Hariri.

Hariri & Hariri designed the bed
and the cabinetry in the master
bedroom using ashwood treated
with white pigment and finished
with lacquer. The plaster walls
are colored with blue pigment.

BUZZ YUDELL

. . . .

Inhabiting a Landscape

BUZZ YUDELL AND TINA BEEBE'S HOUSE in Malibu is as tightly woven into the landscape as the foliage in a medieval tapestry. It is lit by California sunshine and enhanced by the views and scents of the gardens they have cultivated surrounding the house, as well as the more distant outlooks—the Malibu hills to the north and the Pacific Ocean to the south. Outdoor rooms are endowed with as much comfort as the stucco-enclosed rooms of their remarkable house.

In 1976, the couple answered the call of their mentor, Charles Moore, to move from the East to southern California, where Yudell became a partner in the new firm, Moore Ruble Yudell. It remains one of

several collaborative firms Moore established that, in a living legacy to him, continue to produce houses that celebrate habitation. Yudell and Beebe had both worked independently for Moore before they met through him.

Yudell began his studies at Yale just as Moore arrived at the university to serve as the dean of architecture. "Charles was a whimsical radical," Yudell says. "He was like a fresh breeze sweeping in. He made it clear that we were designing places for people." That, and his method of working in collaboration with his clients, were at the time revolutionary ideas. Beebe, a Yale-trained graphic designer, now works for Moore

Ruble Yudell as a color consultant and landscape designer.

When the couple first moved to California, they lived in a 600-square-foot remodeled bungalow and dreamed of building a courtyard house near the beach. They searched along the coast for property they could afford, finally finding a long, skinny lot; no one previously had known what to do with it. The site, 100 feet wide and 600 feet long, was bordered on one side by a dry riverbed and on the other by a neighbor's stables. Restrictions required a 50-foot clearance on the side of the riverbed and 18 feet on the other side for a fire lane. The buildable portion of the property was therefore 600 feet long by 32 feet wide. Real estate agents called the property "distressed," but Yudell and Beebe saw bucolic land that stretched along a gentle slope from the federally protected hills on the north to the view of the Pacific Ocean on the south.

Thinking about how they wanted to live crystallized the couple's memories of houses they felt good in. "We found," Yudell recalls, "it had to do with materials, proportions, light, space, and connection with the landscape. Shaping places for habitation and connection to the land takes precedence over the expression of the object alone." Yudell and Beebe thought of their site, a former tomato farm, as having an essentially agricultural quality, so their design adapts the simple forms of farmhouses they admired in California and southern European countries. It is both an appropriate and economical way to build.

The design emphasizes the strong axes of the site by running a long gallery, wide enough for additional seating, along one side of the generously proportioned main rooms of the house: a kitchen/sitting room and a living/dining room. French doors open the gallery to a paved street that steps down the slope past a series of garden rooms—pergolas, trellises, and a rose court. On the lowest level, a blue lap pool stretches toward the distant view of the Pacific. A staircase to the left of the front door leads up to a hallway that doubles as a library. The master suite, with a sleeping porch that overlooks the view toward the Pacific, occupies one wing off the hall. Beebe's and Yudell's studies are on the opposite side.

"The house does not have the tyranny of a traditional plan," Yudell says. Rather, they have created places that through their character create possibilities, and because many of the rooms open to one another, the plan allows for great flexibility. There is, for example, no formal living room, but a variety of places to dine. Depending on the weather and number of people, meals are taken in the kitchen, living room, or one of the many outdoor rooms; when there is a large party, many of the rooms—both inside and out—are used for dining.

The furnishing of the house is an ongoing collaboration—a process, like the gardens Beebe has planted. She has incorporated some things from her grandparents' house that she finds "comforting," whereas Buzz prefers contemporary designs. Almost all the rooms have an outdoor extension so that the landscape becomes part of the decoration. Beebe, an avid gardener and accomplished cook, fills the house with sumptuous bouquets of flowers. Baskets of fruit and vegetables picked from the gardens and orchards she cultivates soon make their way into aromatic pots in the kitchen. "Gardens," Beebe says, "are a natural extension of architecture and can influence the palette." Under her guidance, color has become an important dimension of the firm's work. It delineates proportions, creates tonal sequences, and imparts light. Beebe worked with the plasterers, mixing the colors on the site and testing how they would look in the location's particular light when they dried. The resulting walls seem to constantly reflect the glow of the California sunset.

LEFT:

Percy laps up the California

sunshine in a gallery paved in

Vicenza limestone that runs the

length of the house. Just to the

left of the entrance, a staircase

leads up to the library. Yudell

made the parchment sconces to

light the first Thanksgiving Day

dinner held at the house.

OPPOSITE:

The gallery steps lead down from

the entry court past the living

spaces. Lounge chairs designed

by Mario Bellini provide

additional seating. A pair of

antique Japanese rice pots stand

on either side of the French

doors. A basket of lemons picked

from the garden sits at the

entrance to the kitchen.

Second Floor Plan

Second Floor Plan
1 Tower
2 Guest Bedroom
3 Study
4 Library
5 Open to Gallery Below
6 Master Bedroom
7 Dressing Room
8 Master Bath
9 Sleeping Porch

Ground Floor Plan

Ground Floor Plan
1 Parking Court
2 Entry Court
3 Entry
4 Gallery
5 Guest Bedroom
6 Pantry
7 Kitchen/Dining
8 Living
9 Pergola
10 Rose Court

Site Plan

Site Plan
1 Olive Grove
2 Pool
3 Pool Court
4 Pergola
5 Rose Court
6 House
7 Entry Court
8 Parking Court
9 Studio/Guest
10 Citrus Orchard

At one end of the living room, an English walnut tilt-top table serves for dining and reading. It stands on a Caucasian rug that belonged to Beebe's grand-parents. The leather chairs are designed by Bellini. On the mantel is a small painting by D. E. May. To either side of the fireplace, the room opens to the adjacent kitchen. Beebe mixed wall colors into the wet plaster as it was applied.

A hallway leading to the master bedroom doubles as a library. It overlooks the gallery on the first floor. A cozy reading corner is decorated with a chair designed by Angelo Donghia and a table by Stephen Sidelinger.

The limestone staircase leads down from the upper level to the gallery. It is decorated with bouquets of garden flowers, a mirror and painted bird from Mexico, and a photograph of Tibet taken by Spencer Beebe.

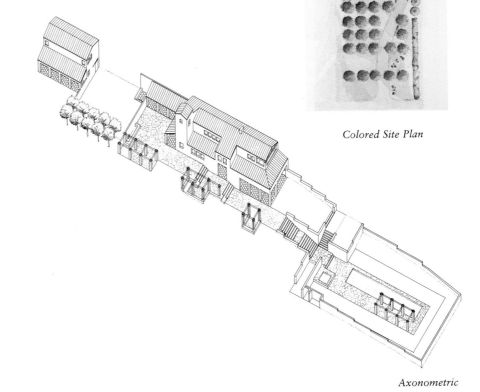

Colored Site Plan

Axonometric

At one end of the kitchen/sitting room, an integral-colored plaster fireplace is ornamented by a simple wooden mantel and verdigris brass trim at the hearth opening. On the mantel, Japanese sake cups stand alongside garden flowers.

In the kitchen, a French cherry table holds old roses, lemons, limes, quinces, and tomatoes from the garden. Small still-life paintings of a walnut and a cherry to either side of the door are by Sally Haley. Dishes inherited from family and collected in travels are displayed on open shelves.

A French fruitwood table
surrounded by wicker armchairs
provides an area for informal

dining. The counter and sink,
used for arranging flowers,
double as a bar for entertaining.

Open shelves hold collections of
antique plates, tureens, and vases,
mixed with new acquisitions.

In the master bath, roses and
anemones from the garden are set
against the watery glow of
integral-colored plaster tile by
Barbara Bead and a celadon slate
floor. Beebe decorated the table
with potato stamps.

The master bedroom opens to a
shaded sleeping porch that looks
toward the Pacific. At one end of
the bedroom are a chaise and
chair that belonged to Beebe's
great-grandmother. The rug is
Caucasian.

In one of the outdoor rooms,

Mexican hammocks are

suspended under a trellised

arcade. Poppies grow between

the paving stones.

A tented poolside cabana creates a room for relaxed entertaining. Figs, freshly picked from the garden, are served with wine and cheese. "The mountains behind and the water in front, especially with the pool between you and the more distant water, give the house wonderful feng shui," Tina says. "It helps collect the good spirits and fool the bad ones so they cannot get in."

MICHAEL RUBIN

. . . .

Designing for Change

"ARCHITECTURE MUST STAND UP to a lot of tests; unless it is flexible and adaptable, it could end up like the dinosaur that became extinct when it had to change its diet," Michael Rubin says. His conviction that a well-designed space should be adaptable to different circumstances has proved successful both in his designs for stores in which merchandise is always changing, and in his decade-long adaptation of a Manhattan industrial space into a comfortable home for a young family.

When Kiki Boucher and Aaron Shipper bought the loft as newlyweds, they intended to convert the space into a home for themselves and their two cats. They chose a floor in a building that had once been a printing plant, located between Greenwich Village and Chelsea in New York City. They liked the idea of living downtown even though the area was almost entirely industrial at the time (now it boasts a number of chic boutiques and restaurants), but they knew it would take time and a good architect to make a home out of that raw space.

"We wanted to keep the feeling of the loft but make it comfortable," Shipper recalls. "And we didn't want a trendy design that would be out of style in six months." After interviewing half a dozen architects, Shipper saw Rubin's work and knew he had found their architect. Rubin is head of his own office in New York City and had already designed several lofts. "No gimmicks, lots of wood and a lack of pretense," is how Shipper sums up his first impression of Rubin's work. Moreover, one of the projects reminded him of the ocean liners his wife loves. Boucher, a Parisian by birth and now a partner in the graphic design firm Drake Boucher, has a finely honed sense of style.

After excess space (about a third of the loft) was partitioned off for rental, Rubin was left with the challenge of 2,300 empty square feet with windows around three sides. "Once I made the decision to place the kitchen in the middle, everything else fell into place," he recalls. The kitchen, enclosed in birch and covered with its own domed roof, resembles a separate little building inserted under the taller loft ceiling. A large, generously windowed area adjoining the kitchen is both dining room and corridor to the living room on one side and master suite on the other. "In Renaissance and baroque architecture, dining rooms were traditionally set up in hallways," Rubin notes.

To retain the character of the loft, Rubin kept the shell intact—columns, ceiling, exterior walls. Then, to "tame" the space, he used elegant materials—pale wood and translucent glass for furniture and for shoji-like screens between the rooms. Tennessee pink marble was used for the floors of the entry, kitchen, dining room, and bathroom. "The training in building materials I received working in Louis Kahn's office has stuck with me," he says. "But this was the first time I personally explored such a rich palette of materials." To heighten the contrast between the domestic apartment and its industrial framework in this space, Rubin had the original exterior walls and columns painted white and the new walls green.

Work proceeded in stages. First the rental apartment was completed, and in due course, Shipper, Boucher, and the two cats moved into their perfectly planned space. Six months later Boucher was pregnant. "Our biggest concern was how to tell Michael he would have to alter the design to accommodate the baby," Shipper says. "But Michael never lost his smile. He simply converted the study next to the living room into a shipshape nursery." Five years later, when a second child was expected, Rubin cut off part of the living room to form another small bedroom.

Over the years, both the space and the furniture Rubin devised for it have adjusted to changes in the family members' lives. Now Philip Shipper likes to pedal his pint-size silver Mercedes around and around

the kitchen, closely followed by his younger brother, Alexander, on his red tricycle. To these children, home is one big piazza. "There are enough restrictions in life without being restricted at home," their mother believes. After having attended several birthday parties there, Rubin comments "It's wonderful to see how the design adapts to having 40 kids running around. A group like that changes the scale of things; the space becomes magical. It's like visiting Oz."

The living-room pocket doors open to the dining room and the corridor that leads to the master bedroom. The V'Soske rug in the living room was designed by Charles Gwathmey. One child-sized chair was found by the owners in Paris, the other in Arizona.

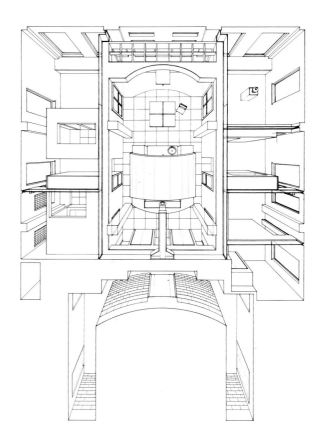

Axonometric

OPPOSITE:

Broad openings provide an expansive spatial flow. With pocket doors open, you can see from the living room, over the breakfast table, to the master bedroom.

Rubin designed the large square dining table on casters so it can be pulled aside when space is needed for large parties. The rug from V'Soske was designed by Anthony Ames; the floor lamps from Delorenzo are by Serge Mouille; the Larsen Loom chairs are from Jack Lenor Larsen.

Looking over the kitchen counter and across the dining table, you can see through the south-facing windows. The shoji screens on the left close off the master bedroom.

The kitchen, seen here from across the dining table, is crafted from birch and has its own arched roof. Murano glass vases and part of the owner's collection of Fiestaware are displayed on the table.

At night the twinkling lights of the towers of the World Trade Center, framed by the center window facing south, form an elegant backdrop for dinner parties.

Translucent glass-and-birch screen and cabinet were designed by Rubin. A Christofle tea set is displayed on the cabinet.

This child's bedroom was once a

study. Its occupant finds it

conveniently close to the kitchen.

Buddy Rubin relaxes in the master bedroom, where the birch-framed, translucent glass screens act as pocket doors that open the room to the dining and living rooms.

Although there is a second small bathroom, the whole family often uses the generously sized master bath, which has two sinks, a large tub, a steam shower enclosed in a glass block, and a toilet in a private cubicle.

STANLEY TIGERMAN
& MARGARET MCCURRY

Accomplishing the Unexpected
Suburban Chicago Residence

ON A QUIET STREET in a Chicago suburb, where traditional-looking houses sit primly behind wide front lawns, a surprising cluster of small, pastel buildings peeks out from behind a wide, circular pink gravel driveway. What appears to be a small village topped by standing-seam zinc roofs sparkling in the sunshine is actually a house designed by architects Stanley Tigerman and Margaret McCurry for a couple with five grown children and a large extended family.

Although Tigerman, a native of Chicago, takes pride in his city's architectural heritage, he was never entirely seduced by either Ludwig Mies van der Rohe's imprint on Chicago or by what was being taught by Paul Rudolph at Yale University's school of architecture, where he was trained. He delights in being unpredictable; whereas many architects of his generation have appropriated a particular style as their signature, the trademark of his work is the unexpected, and the common denominator is surprise. Tigerman credits McCurry, his partner and wife, for making him aware of the importance of interiors. McCurry considers the form, finishes, and furnishings integral to one another, comparing buildings to crystals in which "life takes place inside." The houses they have collaborated on, whether their own small weekend house or more elaborate projects for clients, are enhanced by the point of view each brings to the project. The architecture is enriched by being reflected and embellished by the interior finishes and furnishings.

When you step between the thick columns that flank the entrance to the suburban Chicago house, the sense of being in a village is increased. Instead of entering a traditional foyer, you find yourself on what appears to be a limestone-paved "street" curving through the house. All on one level, the house is,

according to Tigerman, basically a 16-room "ranch burger," but with a twist—each "room" is an autonomous little building with its own roof, and each space has different finishes, lighting, and furnishings, all selected or designed by the architects. This variety infuses the house with an urban excitement.

Just inside the front door are the only totally interior rooms: a round library with rosewood floors, walls, and furniture; a cloakroom with adjoining guest bath; and, to the left, a small cylindrical phone booth, which the owners find handy for private conversations when the house is filled with guests.

Because the other rooms rotate off the main sphere, each is open to views of the pool and gardens in the back. Behind a metal-railed staircase (called the "metro") that leads down to the basement is the hub of the house—a dining room under a flat-roofed, circular drum punctured by a clerestory of small square windows, and surrounded by a circle of silver-painted columns. McCurry says that throughout the house, columns and trim were covered with metallic paint to recall the roofs outside. To accommodate the large family, the room is furnished with three tables, and on Thanksgiving and religious holidays—when as many as 60 sit down to dinner—more tables are set up on the curved "street" outside the colonnade.

Beyond the dining room, the living room is set in a cube covered by a hipped roof that is topped by a light monitor. A large fireplace provides a cozy focus during the long Chicago winters. Come spring, French doors open to the gardens and swimming pool. A rug designed by the architects abstracts the floor plan of the house.

A wedge-shaped media room swings off the living room. Custom cabinets covered in black veneer, which have built-in electronic equipment, provide a striking

contrast to the light-filled living room. McCurry explains that to give the house continuity each room's individual color scheme contains a hint of the color in the next room, thus the white living room is accented with black.

The generously proportioned kitchen was placed at the east end of the house so the family can breakfast in the morning light. The garage used by the owners is opposite the pantry. A small, round sewing room nestles between the garage and kitchen.

The master bedroom suite is beyond the study. Gable-roofed guest rooms are clustered at the west end of the house near the guest garage that stands opposite the driveway from the one used by the owners. This separate garage allows visitors to come and go without passing through other areas of the house.

Black accents in the living room relate to the predominantly black media room to the left of the piano. The green sofa and chairs recall the garden outside the front doors. The living room rug, designed by the architects, abstracts the floor plan of the house, and was custom-fabricated by Spinning Wheel. The forest green sofa is designed by Massimo Iosa Ghin, and the coffee table by Pascal Mourgue; near the entrance to the living room hangs a painting by David Snyder.

Looking toward the entry from behind the stair rail, you see custom-designed glass-topped tables on tubular metal supports flanking the front doors. Square windows outlined with metallic paint pierce the cylinder that encloses the library.

Just inside the front door, across the limestone path, is the door to the cloakroom. The umbrella stand was designed by Marco Zanuso from Luminaire. Sinistra chairs by Paul Haigh from Bernhardt stand in front of staircase that leads down to the basement.

Floor Plan

The fireplace, based on a Count Rumford design, is made of limestone to match the exterior base course of the building. The fireplace screen and tools, designed by the architects, were fabricated by Janet Benes. The pull-up chairs were designed by Mark Mack from Bernhardt.

All the rooms are distinguished by different finishes. Wooden columns covered with metallic paint encompass the oak dining-room floor. Cabinets and the triangular, black-granite-topped dining table are designed by the architects. The rectangular table with wooden top and granite insert is from Stendig, and the Serenissimo table was designed by Lela and Massimo Vignelli/David Law from A.I. The Academy dining chairs were designed by Angelo Donghia.

Each room features a different flooring material. This detail shows the point at which the oak dining-room floor meets the limestone path and the lighter limestone living-room floor. Polished black granite marks a small leftover area between rooms. A stainless steel line designates the back arc of the house from which the rooms spin off.

The cylindrical phone booth that stands on the limestone path just outside the pantry increases the illusion of being on a city street. Woven sisal covers the floor and walls inside the booth. The metal sculpture is by Marcel Flores.

In the master bath, a glass block encloses a shower room, one of two that flank a large tub. The green marble countertops echo the green granite floors and walls.

In the library, cherry shelves, desk, cabinets, and game table are all designed by the architects. Kezu chairs, designed by Dakota Jackson, are upholstered in green leather.

In the master bedroom, the dressing table and pop-up television cabinet were designed by the architects in pale green and blond bird's-eye maple veneer. The French doors opposite the bed open to the garden.

STANLEY TIGERMAN
& MARGARET MCCURRY

. . . .

Accomplishing the Unexpected
Tigerman / McCurry Residence

ALTHOUGH TIGERMAN TOOK CHARGE of the architectural design of the "village" house, with McCurry reinforcing the themes through her furniture and finishing selections, their own small weekend house in a lakeside community in southern Michigan was and continues to be a collaboration. "Neither one of us got entirely what we wanted," Tigerman says. "Yet it is one of our best projects." A tight budget dictated the small size, just 1,000 square feet including the sleeping lofts, and humble materials. The corrugated galvanized sheet-metal walls and standing-seam galvanized sheet-metal roof are part of the local vernacular, materials common to the barns that dot the countryside. The exposed painted plywood ends covered with latticework give the little building a strong geometric impact.

You enter the house by passing alongside the round screen porch directly into the double-height living room, where you face a fireplace flanked by French doors. The geometric grid seen on the outside is repeated on the U-shaped built-in banquette, the window and door mullions, and even the gingham fabric used to cover the seating cushions. Two small bedrooms

are on the left, and the kitchen and bath are on the right. Tigerman credits McCurry with the house's comforting sense of symmetry, and she says he was responsible for the "baroque" embellishments—the curved stairs that lead up to the sleeping loft and the moldings.

Tigerman maintains that, like so much of American architecture, the design of the house is derived from both American and European heritages.

The rectangular building with adjoining round screen porch is reminiscent of a barn and granary, or a basilica and baptistry. The gabled roof, central fireplace, and mullioned windows speak to everyone's image of home. "To Margaret," he says, "it is like a Quaker meetinghouse, while I see it as a Polish shetel."

Seating surrounds the fireplace. *doors flank the fireplace,*

The carved fish and mantel were *reinforcing the room's symmetry.*

worked by a twentieth-century *The tabletop was created by*

Nova Scotia folk artist. French *sculptor Antoni Miralda.*

Steep, round-nosed stairs lead up

to the sleeping lofts that are

tucked below the gabled roof.

Sleeping lofts stand opposite each other at both ends of the double-height living room. A three-sided seating unit, designed by the architects, occupies most of the room in front of a simple white dining table.

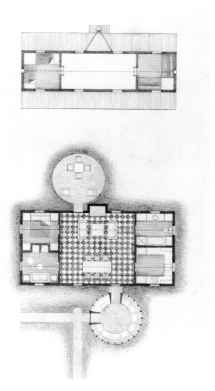

Loft Plan
Floor Plan

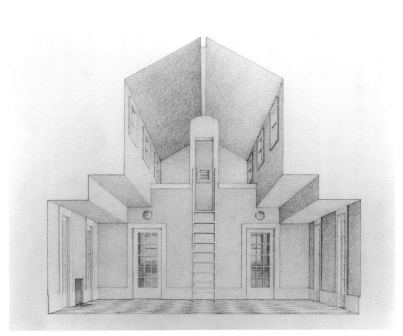

Section

FRANKLIN SALASKY

. . . .

Embellishing a Box

PORTRAITURE IS THE WORD the partners in the New York City–based firm B Five Studio, Architects & Decorators, use to describe their work. At once elegant and eccentric, Franklin Salasky's design for his own 500-square-foot apartment in the Chelsea section of Manhattan is a self-portrait. It displays a finesse that is the result of a very sure hand, and a luxuriousness that belies its small size and relatively tight budget.

When B Five Studio takes on a project, the design often includes architecture, lighting, furnishings, color, and fabrics. "The genesis of the direction of our firm is the idea that it is impossible to separate architecture and decoration," Salasky says. Often they will use architecture as decoration, and decoration to highlight or create architectural details. Salasky credits his comprehensive approach to his training at the Rhode Island School of Design. "It is not just an architecture school," he explains. "There is a concern with the entire material world."

The limits of both the size of his apartment and budget ruled out any great manipulation of the space, so Salasky concentrated on the surfaces and the furnishings. "I realized that I would have to deal with the apartment as a box, so I set out to define it with pattern, color, and texture," he explains. "First, I straightened out the bones of the apartment as judiciously and minimally as possible," he says. He redid the kitchen and created an arched entry between the foyer and the main room. The catalog moldings that give scale to the room were used in a free manner that Salasky says was influenced by Japanese design—which, he explains, also influenced the Victorians. On some walls he placed molding at the traditional chair-rail height, and on others he raised it to head-level. He also used molding to frame the mirror; placed just below the ceiling, it seems to add both depth and height to the space.

Salasky considered dividing the space to create a separate area for the bedroom. Then he saw a bedroom designed by Mario Buatta, the decorator known for his elaborate interiors, and, Salasky says, "something clicked." He decided that if throughout history royalty often entertained in their bedrooms, why shouldn't he? So instead of concealing the bed, he highlighted it, using a column, the canopy, and draperies to define the space.

Typical of the firm's design strategy, Salasky enlisted the aid of artisans to embellish the "box." Mary Bright, whom he describes as "a sculptor in fabric," used a fabric painted by Ted Tyler to produce the bed hangings. Salasky designed the chartreuse bed cover, and Bright executed it. She also made the window treatments. The floor was sanded and then rubbed with paint and urethanes. The hallway was painted by Elliott Levine, who also created the screen that stands in a corner at the far end of the room and painted the fabric for the cloth used on the table near the window.

The apartment reflects Salasky's admiration for the freedom with which the Victorians mixed furniture of different scales and periods, their use of polychromy, and their emphasis on comfort. "This modern concept that decoration is bad is an anomaly that comes from the repudiation of the Victorian style," Salasky says. With a deft hand he has mixed furnishings of his own design (such as the comfortable armchair upholstered in green velvet) with Italian and American designs, predominantly from the 1940s and 1950s. The single room is infused with Salasky's relish for domesticity.

Through the newly built arched
entry from the foyer, you see the
windows at the opposite end of
the apartment. The window
treatment, created by Mary Bright
and Franklin Salasky, conceals the
fact that there are two windows
rather than one. The vintage
Knoll chair was designed by
Pierre Jeanneret. Salasky added
the chartreuse cushions. The tall
ladder-back chairs are attributed
to Gio Ponti.

Bed hangings made by Bright set
the bed apart. An ornate Italian
mirror hangs above the bed. On

the bedside table sits a pineapple-
topped brass lamp. The old

leather sofa is Spanish and dates
from the 1930s.

The room contains a tasteful mix of furnishings designed by the architects, along with choice antiques: the armchair upholstered in green velvet was designed by B Five Studio for Brickel; in front of the chair is a bench designed by Nakashima; behind it is a screen designed by Salasky and painted by Elliott Levine, who also painted the cloth on the table in front of the window. On the table is a glass candelabra by Susan Plum. The mirror, framed in catalog molding, reflects a small painting that Salasky did at age 15. The small wooden table was designed by Gilbert Rohde for Herman Miller. Wallpapers are from Clarence House.

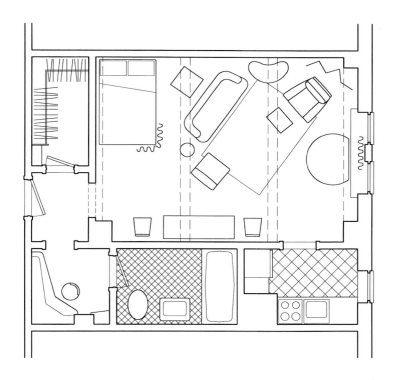

Floor Plan

Salasky transformed a mahogany sideboard, designed by Paul Laszlo but in poor condition, by changing the sliding doors to sycamore and painting the case black. Only the drawers were left with the original mahogany finish. Arranged on the sideboard is a portion of Salasky's collection of Italian ceramics. The taller lamp is French, designed by Jean Royere; the other is Swedish. The painting above the sideboard is by Levine.

A tiny library was built in an alcove off the entrance. The chair was designed by Tom Dixon. A French-style chandelier lights the alcove.

DEBORA REISER

. . . .

Experimenting with Modernism

IN THE BERKSHIRE MOUNTAINS there are still farms with land that has been worked by the same families for generations. The rolling green landscape is punctuated by clusters of small, pitched-roof farm buildings. A Manhattan couple had, for a dozen years,

owned 17 acres of this countryside, but, as the wife says, "I was afraid a house in the country would wind up owning us." She had never wanted one until Debora Reiser renovated their apartment. A onetime professional dancer, the wife found the design process exhilarating and compares the remodeled apartment's light, air, and space to the places she loves best—dance studios. If Reiser could achieve that in a city apartment, it

would be interesting to see what she would do on a former cornfield with a mountain backdrop.

Although Debora Reiser has never veered from modernism, her work has grown increasingly experimental. When she entered Pratt University in 1944, she was one of three women in a class of 75. By the time the class graduated, only 20 students remained, including Reiser. After completing her studies, she spent 25 years working in the office of George Nemeny. "It was there that I got used to doing everything," Reiser says. "We designed the furniture, lighting, and rugs. The problem with architecture in this country is that it is often treated as a business rather than an art." Since leaving Nemeny's office, Reiser has headed her own firm, where she has for years been producing impeccably crafted work in the modernist tradition, including the Manhattan couple's apartment and the renovation of a house for the husband's brother just across the road from the property they owned.

"Debora is interested in what her clients want but is mature enough to direct them," the wife says. The couple's requirements for the house were specific: three bedrooms; a studio for him; a kitchen for her—separate but not completely closed off from the living and dining rooms, so that she could see and hear what was going on while preparing meals; lots of windows; and a screened porch. The wife loves space and hates clutter, but she worried about how neighbors would react to a spare modern house in the midst of their bucolic New England landscape. "My husband didn't want the neighbors saying, 'Those New Yorkers came in and ruined everything,'" she recalls.

To fulfill the couple's wish list for the house without offending the neighbors, Reiser fragmented the house's 5,000 square feet into several clusters. The main volumes, enclosed in white vertical siding under pitched

roofs of cedar shakes, are not unlike neighboring farm buildings, but a contemporary glass-and-painted stucco link connects the main portion of the house (living and dining rooms and master bedroom suite) to the two additional bedrooms, which are topped by a studio. "The kitchen pivots off the dining room into the view of the woods like a bird's wing," Reiser explains. A back hall leads from the kitchen to an open court that connects the house to the garage.

Large expanses of glass doors and windows open the house to outdoor views. When visitors step inside the front door, they see the swimming pool through the living room's back wall of glass doors; the wife, who loves the beach, has her water view, as well as the Berkshire Mountains in the background. A glass-enclosed gallery, with outdoor views framed by large red columns, runs the length of the living room to the dining room on the right, and the master bedroom on the left. To emphasize the connection between the interior of the house and the outdoors, Reiser used the same bluestone flooring in the living room, gallery, kitchen, and terraces. The floors are radiantly heated to increase the owners' pleasure in walking barefoot. In the tradition of the early modernists, Reiser designed much of the furniture for the house, including the dining and coffee tables, all three beds, the living room rug, and the aluminum chandeliers in the living room. She also helped select the fabrics and antiques.

The couple got everything they asked for except the screened porch, and because the house so embraces the outdoors, they don't miss it. "The entire house is like a screened porch," the wife says.

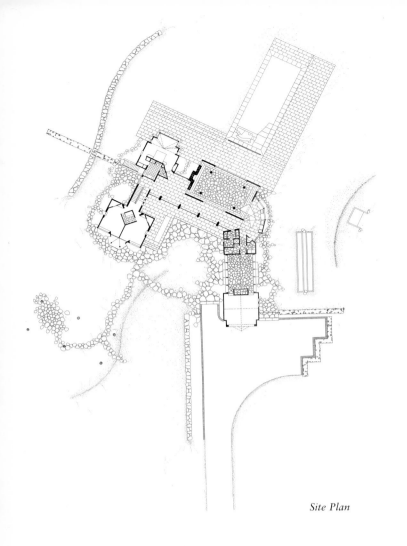

Site Plan

The gallery runs along the length of the living room and dining room to the master bedroom suite on one side and the kitchen on the other. It connects the rooms to the outdoors through a wall of windows punctuated by three-foot-wide red columns. "I used the columns to frame the views and to prevent the house from looking as wide-open as a supermarket," Reiser says. A Shaker school desk holds part of the owners' hat collection.

Roof caps, collected locally, stand on pedestals designed by Reiser at the end of the gallery near the *master bedroom. Antique game boards hang above the Shaker desk.*

A glass and painted-stucco link connects the main portion of the house to the wing that contains the two guest bedrooms and the studio upstairs.

The fireplace at the end of the living room was made of local stones from tumbled stone walls that once marked the boundaries of New England farms. Chairs by Bruce Eicher surround the dining table.

Sliding glass doors open the living room to the pool and the view of the Berkshire Mountains. The pool and landscape were designed by the firm of Debora's son and daughter-in-law, Reiser/Umemoto Architects. Reiser designed the aluminum chandeliers and the mahogany dining and coffee tables. The row of small, square, highly placed windows brings additional light into the room. The concrete columns are structural.

A glass-enclosed sitting area of
the master bedroom looks
toward the view of the
Berkshires.

The kitchen is topped by a roof that Reiser describes as shaped like a parasol. An island with marble counter provides a generously proportioned work space. Attached to it is an ash block table. The back hall opens to the court that connects the house to the garage.

In one of the guest bedrooms, a

cherry pencil-post bed designed

by Reiser is covered by a late-

nineteenth-century log cabin–

patterned quilt.

A mahogany staircase with painted-steel handrail leads up to the studio. Sheetrock walls are painted to resemble the exterior stucco.

In a guest bedroom, Reiser's contemporary version of a sleigh bed, produced in aluminum, is covered with a Lancaster County Amish nine-patch quilt.

WALTER CHATHAM

. . . .

Reinventing Regionalism

WALTER CHATHAM TOOK ON a formidable challenge when he decided to transform an abandoned power plant, one of the few untouched spaces left in Manhattan's SoHo neighborhood, into a home for his wife and three young children. Chatham, an architect who heads his own firm in New York City, has designed numerous Manhattan interiors, as well as projects in the Caribbean and at Seaside, Florida, where his work has been influenced by the local vernacular.

Chatham studied architecture at the University of Maryland, but he believes an important part of his education took place when he took a year off to work for the Miami-based firm Arquitectonica. While working there, he had the job of driving to the airport to meet architects invited to speak at a club in the city. His views were broadened by getting to know the luminaries he escorted to and from the airport. More recently, in his capacity as president of New York City's Architectural League, Chatham has brought some of the world's leading architects to speak in Manhattan.

Nevertheless, Chatham believes the single most influential development in his career was the study of vernacular housing he did for the first house he designed. In 1981, when his wife's parents asked him to design a house for them on the island of Nevis, Chatham looked at native housing for a model, and since then he always examines local buildings to see what works in a particular climate and what will fit well in a given region.

By the time Chatham took on the renovation of the power plant, he had extensive experience designing interior renovations in Manhattan. Although he admires the work of the early modernists and believes that "modernism is New York's regional vernacular," he has come to distrust style "isms": "Classification tends to exclude other options." Moreover, Chatham says, "Living with children has had a profound effect upon my work. They have completely destroyed my

desire for glass doors."

He and his wife, designer Mary Adams Chatham, were pioneers when they moved to SoHo, almost two decades ago, long before the area bristled with fancy shops and restaurants. With the arrival of their children, they expanded their original loft to include an additional floor of their building. The children and their nanny occupied the top level, and a small elevator connected them to the parents' rooms below. Life on two levels, and the awkward time lapse caused by the elevator, became too complicated, and before long the Chathams were loft hunting again.

"After seeing a lot of renovations, we chose this space because it had never been renovated; it was totally raw, totally pure," says Mary Adams Chatham about the top floor of the abandoned power plant. What the couple considered "pure," most people would consider a wreck. The space had been on the market for 15 years. The Chathams not only saw the possibilities for renovation but also didn't want to totally lose the sense of what had been there before. So they kept the concrete floor and the original beams, encasing them in sheetrock. The team assembled by Chatham and contractor Tony Lee managed to complete the renovation in just two and a half months while Mary and the children were out of town for the summer.

Although all five Chathams share one floor, "to put some distance between the generations" Chatham organized the space to make a separate area for the children at the entrance. Here a $7\frac{1}{2}$-by-35-foot hall that serves as gym and playroom is flanked by three ship's-quarters-size bedrooms and a bath. A well-equipped kitchen and dining area can be closed off from the children's space with tall metal doors. The master bedroom, with an antique bed strategically placed so the couple can survey their entire realm from bed, is at the opposite end of the loft from the children's space. Just outside the master bedroom at one end of the living

room, a bright orange, metal staircase leads up to Mary's studio and the roof garden.

Furnishings are a mix of inherited pieces, things the Chathams have collected, and their own designs. "If I cannot find a perfect piece of furniture, I design it," Mary Adams Chatham says. Although the couple shares an impressive knowledge of the history of architecture and design, Chatham says, "living with our children is teaching me to operate more intuitively. Experimenting with color and light is the most joyful thing about being an architect. I would like to think that if someone from a culture totally removed from our own, with no knowledge of our architecture, visited one of my projects, he would like my work."

The entrance hallway doubles as a playroom for the children. The glass-topped table was designed by their mother, Mary Adams Chatham. The synthetic-blend carpets are machine-washable. The drawing above the table is by David Winter.

As a reminder of the power
station that originally occupied
the space, Chatham painted the
metal staircase bright orange. It
leads up to the studio and the
roof garden.

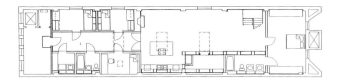

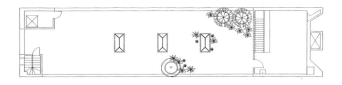

Floor Plan

Sections

In the living room, gray chairs

with tubular metal frames were

designed by Warren McArthur.

The watercolor above the

fireplace was done by

Aldo Rossi.

"The kitchen and dining area act as a buffer zone between the children's loft and the adults' space," Chatham says. Since the youngest child's room did not have an outside window, she was given a view to the kitchen through a window from Urban Archaeology.

Pell chairs from the 1930s

surround aluminum and

lacquered fiberboard tables

designed by Jonas Milder.

The painting on the right is

by Pier Luigi Consagra.

The antique bed belonged to

Walter Chatham's mother.

Curtains and bed hangings are by

Mary Bright. The harlequin

dressing table was designed by

Mary Adams Chatham.

A study is formed from a small

space tucked behind the living

room. Bookshelves painted

bright yellow line the wall of

the living room.

LEE MINDEL

. . . .

Uniting Architecture with Decoration

AN IDYLLIC SHINGLE-COVERED COTTAGE with a wide porch, rose-covered trellised courtyard, separate dining pavilion, and guest quarters, Lee Mindel's weekend house looks like a miniature of the posh turn-of-the-century estates on the other side of the railroad tracks in Southampton, New York. It is hard to

believe that the house started out as a two-room asbestos-sided shack. The new owner, Lee Mindel, is a partner with Peter Shelton in the Manhattan architecture firm of Shelton, Mindel and Associates. Although the firm is best known for grand projects such as elegant apartments overlooking Central Park, interiors for major art collectors, and the corporate headquarters for Polo Ralph Lauren, the transformation of Mindel's 1,600-square-foot house is in many ways representative of their work. Architecture and decoration are approached as a seamless discipline, with meticulous

attention to detail; outdoors and indoors merge to make small spaces seem larger; gardens become rooms open to the sky; and antiques are deftly mixed with furniture designed by the architects and objects from contemporary craftspeople.

Shelton and Mindel met when they were both students at the University of Pennsylvania. Mindel continued his studies at the Harvard Graduate School of Design, Shelton at Pratt Institute. They met again in New York City, where they were working for large firms on huge projects. Their mutual desire for work with which they could feel a more personal connection resulted in their forming a partnership to launch their own firm in 1978. When Shelton, Mindel and Associates takes on a project, whether large or small, no detail escapes attention. Their design for an apartment renovation will typically include a restructuring of the interior space, including walls, floors, and ceilings; the custom design of rugs and furnishings; and the selection of antiques, bed linens, and even accessories. "Historically, architecture and interiors were conceived as a single entity, from Andrea Palladio to Frank Lloyd Wright and Le Corbusier by way of Robert Adam," says Shelton. In addition to interiors for grand Manhattan apartments, suburban houses, and corporate offices, the firm has designed furniture, rugs, and lighting.

In Shelton, Mindel's designs, structure often becomes ornament, and ornaments enforce and reflect structure. For example, the scale for the renovation of an apartment in Manhattan for art collectors was dictated by 10-by-15-foot paintings and floor-to-ceiling sculpture. In that apartment, art and structure merge so seamlessly that paintings seem to divide the space, and the structure appears to be sculpture.

The firm's work often reveals an intentional ambiguity in the definition of interior and outdoor space. Walls open to reveal gardens. Gardens are mirrored in the design of carpets. In Mindel's weekend house, all unnecessary walls were removed, and the dining pavilion and guest house were set a few feet apart. A view of the outdoors from every room creates the illusion that the house is larger. In a suburban house in which only the front received light, they cut a steel-framed, skylit corridor through the entire house to bring in light. This tendency to pull apart structural elements has sometimes caused Shelton, Mindel's work to be labeled deconstructivist. Yet their interiors also display a traditional concern for comfort, the elegance of luxurious fabrics, and exquisite craftsmanship. According to Mindel, although some projects may have traditional aspects, the firm's approach is always modernist. They use their knowledge of history to abstract ideas, employ the latest technology, and apply the modernist's open plan in new and often innovative ways. Yet every project is unique. The variety of the firm's work makes it difficult to pin a label on their style, which is perhaps as it should be. Mindel says, "The style is the penmanship with which you write the thesis. There must be a deeper idea present."

Although Mindel has filled his country house with an assortment of antiques that look as if they had been collected by several generations of a particularly stylish family, he also has some very up-to-date modern designs. The staircase without a railing looks like a contemporary sculpture, and the rooms open to one another and the outdoors in a decidedly modern way. As with many of their projects, the site posed a major challenge and also suggested the solution. Decades ago, when developers divided up the area's potato farms into suburban neighborhoods, they created "flag lots." Houses are set back from the street with long driveways, shared by neighbors, at the edge of their property. The long driveway enabled Mindel, on the advice of landscape architect Nancy Haseley, to create a dramatic entrance. It divides the front garden and then appears to cut

through the house like a street bisecting a village. The front gardens lead to a rose-covered trellised court with a brilliant blue lap pool, which during the day reflects light into the living room and dining pavilion. Illuminated at night, it looks like a giant rectangular aquamarine set in the dark green garden.

A round English regency fruitwood breakfast table is surrounded by William IV chairs. Above the table is an English 1920s lighting fixture with a shade designed by Mindel. A clock created by the London designer Andre Dubreuil hangs on the staircase. The hammered sheet-metal side table is also one of Dubreuil's designs.

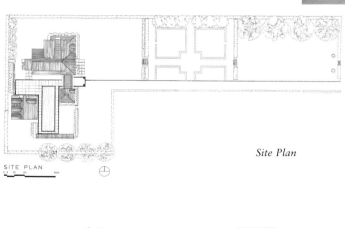

Site Plan

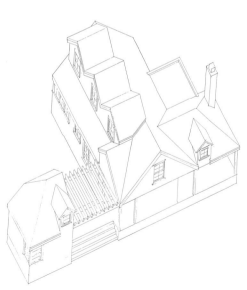

Axonometric

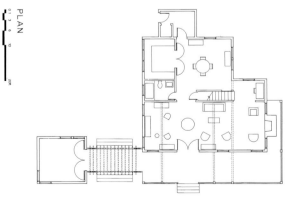

Floor Plan

In the living room, creamy white walls and light, polished floors provide a clean backdrop for Mindel's quirky mix of antique furniture, mostly found in flea markets. At the far end of the room, tall windows are framed by simple, unlined linen curtains. In front of the windows, an English regency recamier is flanked by two pedestals designed by Mindel: the pedestal on the left supports a sculpture by Mark Brazier-Jones, the other a porcelain maquette by an unknown artist. The round mahogany empire table holds a bouquet of garden flowers. The late-nineteenth-century fruitwood bookcase displays part of Mindel's collection of creamware. The deep English smoking chair on the left is covered in a nineteenth-century French fabric. A pair of English busts of German musicians rests on bookcases to each side of the front door. Mindel says the busts are a "nod to the context"; the garden of the Parish Museum in Southampton is filled with similar plaster statues. An American gothic revival table stands in front of a slipper chair upholstered in blue stripes.

The wide, white wood-and-oak staircase doubles as a divider between the dining and living rooms. A gothic chair stands on the landing.

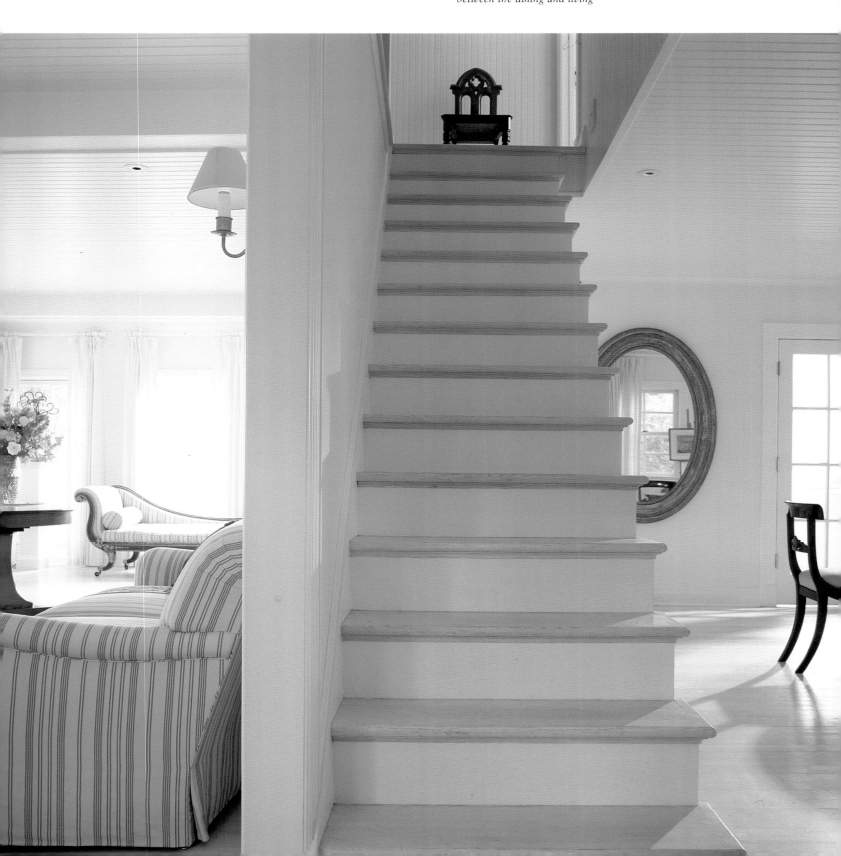

On the second floor, a narrow hallway stretches above the open stairway. Along the wall in the hallway stands a gothic sewing table.

At the far end of the master bedroom, a small sitting area is tucked beneath the exposed beams of the roof gable. Bead-center-bead paneling adds to the room's allusions to vintage details. On the left a Biedermeier pedestal holds a fruit bowl. On the right a Coad stone bust reposes on the French provincial chest of drawers. Two small 1920s Liberty stools sit in front of the window. The William IV library chair on the left is upholstered in blue-and-white-striped fabric; the small William IV chair on the right is covered in a floral chintz.

Exposed sheathing and framing
give the pavilion a relaxed, rustic
feeling. In summer it is used as a
dining and sitting room.
Furnishings were found at flea
markets and country shops.

Sophie, the owner's springer
spaniel, reposes in the guest room
alongside a mahogany empire
bed. The William IV chair is
upholstered in blue-and-white

ticking. A collection of
eighteenth-century engravings,
colored in the nineteenth century,
is propped on the floor.

The stairway in the guest house rises alongside a wall paneled with birch plywood. Southampton tax maps hang above the panels.

The balcony of the guest house serves as a dormitory. At the far end, a 1920s Biedermeier revival chest holds a collection of Etrurian ware.

A bird's-eye view of the guesthouse, taken from the second floor, shows an art nouveau hooked needlepoint rug beneath a Biedermeier table. A Victorian storage bench covered in a Hungarian drapery fabric sits below a large American gothic mirror from a church school. The English sofa is upholstered in a paisley from Fonthill. Mindel found the 1940s torchere, to the left of the sofa, at an auction-house tag sale.

DAVID BAKER

. . . .

Crafting a Collage

DAVID BAKER ARRIVED in Berkeley, California, in 1971 with a knapsack on his back and never left. He now heads his own architectural firm in San Francisco, but still lives across the bay in Berkeley. "I like a building to be a collage, with overlaps and collisions that tell a story," he says. Baker often names his projects. His own house, which he designed in collaboration with architect Nancy Whitcombe, has a title as quirky as its appearance: House of the Stuccoids. The inspiration for the design came to Baker and Whitcombe from the science fiction movie *Day of the Triffids*, in which alien, mobile plants called triffids attack and destroy most of humanity. According to Baker, the house, with its flat-roofed, boxy, stucco blocks that appear to collide into a wood facade, narrates the march of the "Stuccoids," the stucco bungalows of the flatlands, up the Berkeley hills to battle the "Maybecks," the eclectic wood-clad houses designed by Bernard Ralph Maybeck in the early 1900s, which greatly influenced California architecture.

Baker grew up in a house that was an architectural experiment—a solar adobe house designed by his father, a self-trained architect who had been a Dutch migrant farmworker. The house was scheduled for publication in *Arts and Architecture* magazine until they discovered that Baker Senior was not a licensed architect. Surrounded by the tools of the trade and art and architecture publications, the son says his professional destiny was determined at an early age. Three years after Baker hitchhiked to Berkeley, he entered the University of California's architecture program. Before graduating, Baker and two friends won a state-sponsored competition for energy-efficient, affordable housing. That project led to others and the formation of Sol-Arc, a firm specializing in affordable housing and energy consultancy.

In 1982, tired of doing research and writing reports, Baker established his own firm, which has pro-

duced a diversity of projects, including award-winning affordable housing, conversions of industrial buildings to residences, trendy cafes, and university interiors. For both his residential and commercial projects, Baker seeks the participation of Bay Area artisans, including furniture designers, woodworkers, metalsmiths, steel fabricators, and mosaic artisans. His ability to incorporate the work of a variety of craftspeople into a design that remains distinctly his own is evident in the House of the Stuccoids.

Baker, who was a carpenter before becoming an architect, did much of the work on the house himself and designed all the built-ins, including the wardrobe in the master bedroom, the home office, the buffet in the dining area, some of the furniture, and his most unusual experiment—the kitchen. The plan of the house is casual, but almost all the furniture is custom-made and the surfaces embellished by craftspeople. Baker favors materials like copper and stucco that gain a patina with age and use. "If I were Louis XIV I could keep things perfect, but as it is, I would rather see the marks of wear," he says.

The house is built on what Baker describes as a "leftover" lot, 3,000 square feet with an 18-foot grade, where the streets of Berkeley meet the Claremont Canyon Regional Preserve. The three-bedroom house steps up the steep hillside with seven half-levels linked by an angled plan. To serve their casual lifestyle, Baker and Whitcombe arranged the main rooms of the house on the entry level—living, dining, kitchen, and home office—into one "great room" defined by different heights and materials. Baker, who likes to cook, left the kitchen open to the living and dining areas so he can chat with family and guests while preparing a meal. In what he describes as an "ad hoc postindustrial response," the kitchen is marked off from the living room by three steel posts to which a cooking range, chopping block, cookbook holder, knife magnet bar,

microwave, and pot rack are attached with adjustable clamps. A special crank allows the range to be easily raised or lowered. The three bedrooms, two baths, and utility room are stacked in the upper levels, connected by a staircase that twists up the tower, which pokes out of the building. Terraces, shaded by live oak trees, extend the rooms, some of which have views over Berkeley to San Francisco Bay.

The house's continuation of the arts and crafts tradition and its trellises and indoor/outdoor areas all reflect the influence of Bay Area architecture, as does its spirit of experimentation. "I like to regard my work as a bubbling stew. It is the lack of resolution that gives the projects energy," Baker says.

Mosaic artist Twyla Arthur found
the Saarinen table at a junk sale
and reconstructed it. She also
refinished the dining chairs.

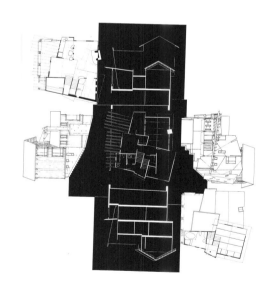

First Floor Plan
Second Floor Plan
Third Floor Plan

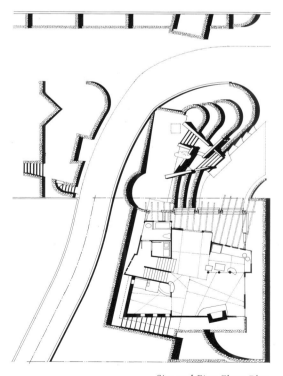

Site and First Floor Plan

Just inside the front door is the dining area of Baker's "great room." The buffet was designed by Baker and executed by woodworker Paco Prieto. It is made of maple plywood with a zinc top. The glass inset is by Mary White. The floor is polished, stained concrete.

In Baker's innovative kitchen, the range, a cutting board, and microwave oven are attached to steel posts with clamps that may be adjusted to the height of the cook. Baker made the aniline-dyed box that contains the microwave, attached to the post on the left. The wooden lounge was designed by Jim Zack. Arthur made the top for the old typing table using pieces of glass rescued from the Oakland fire.

Baker tucked a home office into one end of the "great room." On the first landing of the staircase is a forged bronze railing that Baker collaborated on with Michael Bondi, an art black-smith. The red chair was designed by Max Leiber, the leather and metal bench by Tom Jameson.

LEFT:

On the back wall of a landing in the stair tower, working quickly before the plaster dried, Arthur and Whitcombe arranged Whitcombe's seashell collection and hardware from Arthur's father's store.

Baker designed the bathroom cabinet to hold books and magazines as well as the usual essentials. Arthur was responsible for the mosaics. The 1948 sink was salvaged.

The second bath is also enhanced by Arthur's mosaics.

The stained-plywood wardrobe
in the master bedroom was
designed by Baker and built
by Paco Pietro. Pietro admires
Baker's ability to blend
"craftspeople's expertise into
his own palette."

In the master bath, Arthur
created the tub surround with
concrete tile made by Buddy
Rhodes. Treetops shade the
corner window.

PETER PENNOYER

· · · · · · ·

Adding Innovation to Tradition

"HOUSES ARE MY FAVORITE PROJECTS," Peter Pennoyer says. In a partnership with Peter Moore, Pennoyer did commercial work for fashion designers and artists such as Keith Haring and Zoran; in association with his former firm, Pennoyer Turino Architects, he completed numerous large residential and institutional projects, including the award-winning renovation of The Mark, a residential apartment hotel in Manhattan. Yet Pennoyer believes that "designing a house is the complete architectural experience. There is the relationship with history, with the client, and with the site. Everything about architecture is in a house; every room may be sculpted to make it a different experience."

When the architect was 34 years of age, his parents asked him to design a house for them. The commission presented him with an opportunity to do a

complete project—the architecture, landscape, and interiors. The site, which is at the end of a two-mile-long peninsula on Mishaum Point at the southeastern corner of Massachusetts, commands a sweeping view east

across Buzzards Bay to Cape Cod and the Elizabeth Islands. The point was settled as farmland in the late 1600s. Now summer houses mingle with the remaining farms. Pennoyer's mother summered down the road from this property in a turn-of-the-century shingled house, which has remained in their family. According to Pennoyer, that house inspired the basic massing of his scheme: a gabled shed set parallel to the shore and wrapped with low, spreading verandas.

For the design of the new house, Pennoyer sought inspiration from two sources. Whereas the sweeping porches, dormers, shingled facade, and gabled mass are in the tradition of the area's shingled houses, the interiors are infused with classical proportions and detailing. From the outside, only the double-height bay window facing the garden and the arched elevation of the living room that looks toward the bay refer to the classical spirit of the interior of the house.

Just inside the front door, an arched transom marks the entry to the living room. This arch is repeated in the windows above the living room's French doors and in the opening to a study raised half a level. The cornice that supports the arches wraps all of the major rooms. Pennoyer had the panel above the cornice wallpapered with a design by William Morris.

A large oriel occupies almost the entire wall of the study. It faces west, opening the center of the house to the afternoon light and breezes. This bay window commands an axis that runs through the house into a garden and ends with a toolshed that Pennoyer designed as "a folly, part Palladian, part rustic, whose miniature scale makes the garden seem far larger than it is." The study is open to the living room below, as well as to a hall on the second floor. The study also serves as a landing for the staircase that connects all three levels.

In contrast to the living room's elaborately coffered ceiling and classical detailing, the furnishings are relaxed and simple. The main rooms were all painted

white to contrast with the William Morris–designed wallpaper above the cornice and to emphasize their intricate paneling and moldings. The bedrooms, however, were each given a specific color scheme. When Pennoyer was studying architecture at Columbia, "many of the critics were put off by plans that seemed too comfortable and would furnish well," he says. In contrast, Robert A. M. Stern taught him that the design of houses "begins with suggesting a way of living."

Because his parents were eager for the house to be completed in time for the summer season, he had only three months to install the interiors. Pennoyer, working with his wife, Katie Ridder, an interior designer, managed within a relatively small budget and the tight time frame to create the sort of casually elegant interiors that usually reflect decades of collecting. Pennoyer selected furniture, reproduction porcelains, screens, and fabrics that he and Katie had found in their travels in the East. "There is long tradition of Oriental furniture being compatible with shingle-style architecture," Pennoyer says. To stretch the budget, Pennoyer's office designed some of the furniture and all the built-in lighting themselves. "The custom-designed furniture, from the low center table in the living room to the shelf units in the green bedroom, which incorporate Indonesian mats, also evokes the Oriental furniture favored by the shingle-style architects," Pennoyer says. The interiors illustrate his propensity for combining a respect for tradition with innovative design.

Furnishings were intentionally kept casual in the classically detailed living room. "In general, the furniture was chosen for its simplicity and materiality," Pennoyer says. He designed the zebrawood coffee table. The Chinese bamboo side chairs, the Chinese porcelains, and the sofas and club chairs are upholstered in J. H. Thorpe and Company's "Province Duck." The striped sisal rug is from Pottery Barn.

*The front hall arches frame the
entrance to the living room,
where French doors open to a
terrace facing the water. The
wallpaper above the cornice is
the "Chrysanthemum" pattern
designed by William Morris.*

*A bay window in the study brings
light and breezes through an open
balcony to the living room below.
Behind the sofa is a reproduction
of a Japanese Edo period screen.
A sugarcane crusher serves as an
end table next to the sofa.*

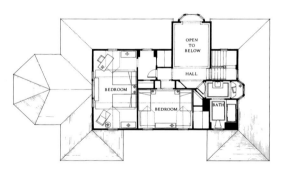

SECOND FLOOR PLAN

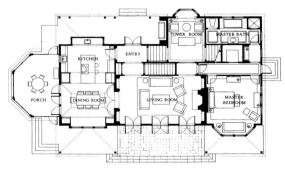

GROUND FLOOR PLAN

The dining room is open to the kitchen, but its higher ceiling, shaped like a truncated pyramid and painted a smoky blue, defines it as a separate space. The antique dining table is from the Philippines. Because kitchens are often the center of activity in summer houses, Pennoyer designed this one to easily accommodate two people working with others gathered around. The same oak flooring is used in the kitchen and dining room; kitchen cabinets are wood with maple interiors.

"Everything was designed to breathe with the sea air and to look even better when it is old and used," Pennoyer says.

The oriel in the study looks out onto a garden designed by Pennoyer with Madison Cox. From the beginning, Pennoyer envisioned the oriel focusing on a garden. "It created the opportunity to do a formal garden in the ragtag landscape," he says.

Pennoyer describes the center yellow bedroom as more "anchored," because you don't see the view until you are in bed. Obi panels were made up into curtains that hang in front of the doorway so that on a hot night the door can be left open to help circulate the air. Pennoyer designed the headboards; the table lamps are from Lights Up; the checked sisal rug is from Pottery Barn.

The two upstairs bedrooms are shaped by the folded planes of the pitched-roof dormers. In contrast to the downstairs, detailing was intentionally kept simple. The pine table, desk chair, and bouclé rug are all from Pottery Barn.

For his parents, who love big, old bathrooms, Pennoyer designed the upstairs bathroom to have two exposures. Under one of the windows he placed a dressing table.

Upstairs, a mirror reflects a hall

that extends from the staircase

across the house to the "green"

bedroom overlooking the bay.

Just inside the door to the green

bedroom is a bureau built by

Courtney Bird to Pennoyer's

design. He describes it as "shelves

rigged up with mats as cover."

DIRECTORY OF ARCHITECTS

. . . .

David Baker
David Baker Associates Architects
461 Second Street
Suite C127
San Francisco, CA 94107

Darcy Bonner
Darcy Bonner & Associates
205 West Wacker Drive, #307
Chicago, IL 60606

Walter Chatham
Walter F. Chatham, A.I.A.,
Architects
524 Broadway #601
New York, NY 10012

Michael Graves
Michael Graves Architect
341 Nassau Street
Princeton, NJ 08540-4692

Charles Gwathmey
Gwathmey Siegel & Associates
Architects
475 Tenth Avenue
New York, NY 10018

Gisue Hariri and Mojgan Hariri
Hariri & Hariri Architects
18 East 12th Street
New York, NY 10003

Scott Himmel
Scott Himmel Architects
205 West Wacker Drive, #309
Chicago, IL 60606

James Hong
James Hong Design
99 Stanton Street
New York, NY 10002

Hugh Newell Jacobsen
Hugh Newell Jacobsen, F.A.I.A.
Architect
2529 P Street NW
Washington, DC 20007-3024

Lee Mindel
Shelton, Mindel & Associates
216 West 18th Street
New York, NY 10011

Charles Moore and Arthur
Andersson
Moore/Andersson Architects, Inc.
2102 Quarry Road
Austin, TX 78703

Peter Pennoyer
Peter Pennoyer Architects P.C.
1239 Broadway, Penthouse
New York, NY 10001

Debora K. Reiser
Debora K. Reiser Design Associates
28 South Washington Avenue
Dobbs Ferry, NY 10522

Michael Rubin
Michael Rubin Architects
200 Park Avenue South
New York, NY 10003

Franklin Salasky
B Five Studio, LLP
160 Fifth Avenue
Suite 702
New York, NY 10010

Frederic Schwartz
Anderson/Schwartz Archtects
180 Varick Street
New York, NY 10014

Stanley Tigerman and Margaret
McCurry
Tigerman McCurry Architeccts
444 North Wells Street
Chicago, IL 60610

Joseph Valerio
Valerio Dewalt Train Associates
200 North LaSalle
Suite 2400
Chicago, IL 60601

Robert Venturi and Denise Scott
Brown
Venturi, Scott Brown and
Associates, Inc.
4236 Main Street
Philadelphia, PA 19127

Buzz Yudell
Moore Ruble Yudell Architects
& Planners
933 Pico Boulevard
Santa Monica, CA 90405